Activated Carbon Adsorption of Trace Organic Compounds

U.S. Environmental Protection Agency

The BiblioGov Project is an effort to expand awareness of the public documents and records of the U.S. Government via print publications. In broadening the public understanding of government and its work, an enlightened democracy can grow and prosper. Ranging from historic Congressional Bills to the most recent Budget of the United States Government, the BiblioGov Project spans a wealth of government information. These works are now made available through an environmentally friendly, print-on-demand basis, using only what is necessary to meet the required demands of an interested public. We invite you to learn of the records of the U.S. Government, heightening the knowledge and debate that can lead from such publications.

Included are the following Collections:

Budget of The United States Government
Presidential Documents
United States Code
Education Reports from ERIC
GAO Reports
History of Bills
House Rules and Manual
Public and Private Laws

Code of Federal Regulations
Congressional Documents
Economic Indicators
Federal Register
Government Manuals
House Journal
Privacy act Issuances
Statutes at Large

Environmental Protection Technology Series

ACTIVATED CARBON ADSORPTION OF TRACE ORGANIC COMPOUNDS

Municipal Environmental Research Laboratory
Office of Research and Development
U.S. Environmental Protection Agency
Cincinnati, Ohio 45268

RESEARCH REPORTING SERIES

Research reports of the Office of Research and Development, U.S. Environmental Protection Agency, have been grouped into nine series. These nine broad categories were established to facilitate further development and application of environmental technology. Elimination of traditional grouping was consciously planned to foster technology transfer and a maximum interface in related fields. The nine series are:

1. Environmental Health Effects Research
2. Environmental Protection Technology
3. Ecological Research
4. Environmental Monitoring
5. Socioeconomic Environmental Studies
6. Scientific and Technical Assessment Reports (STAR)
7. Interagency Energy-Environment Research and Development
8. "Special" Reports –
9. Miscellaneous Reports

This report has been assigned to the ENVIRONMENTAL PROTECTION TECHNOLOGY series. This series describes research performed to develop and demonstrate instrumentation, equipment, and methodology to repair or prevent environmental degradation from point and non-point sources of pollution. This work provides the new or improved technology required for the control and treatment of pollution sources to meet environmental quality standards.

This document is available to the public through the National Technical Information Service, Springfield, Virginia 22161.

EPA-600/2-77-223
December 1977

ACTIVATED CARBON ADSORPTION OF
TRACE ORGANIC COMPOUNDS

by

Vernon L. Snoeyink, John J. McCreary and Carol J. Murin
Department of Civil Engineering
University of Illinois
Urbana, Illinois 61801

Grant No. R 803473

Project Officer

Alan A. Stevens
Water Supply Research Division
Municipal Environmental Research Laboratory
Cincinnati, Ohio 45268

MUNICIPAL ENVIRONMENTAL RESEARCH LABORATORY
OFFICE OF RESEARCH AND DEVELOPMENT
U.S. ENVIRONMENTAL PROTECTION AGENCY
CINCINNATI, OHIO 45268

DISCLAIMER

This report has been reviewed by the Municipal Environmental Research Laboratory, U.S. Environmental Protection Agency, and approved for publication. Approval does not signify that the contents necessarily reflect the views and policies of the U.S. Environmental Protection Agency, nor does mention of trade names or commercial products constitute endorsement or recommendation for use.

FOREWORD

The Environmental Protection Agency was created because of increasing public and government concern about the dangers of pollution to the health and welfare of the American people. Noxious air, foul water, and spoiled land are tragic testimony to the deterioration of our natural environment. The complexity of that environment and interplay between its components require a concentrated and integrated attack on the problem.

Research and development is that necessary first step in problem solution and it involves defining the problem, measuring its impact, and searching for solutions. The Municipal Environmental Research Laboratory develops new and improved technology and systems for the prevention, treatment, and management of wastewater and solid and hazardous waste pollutant discharges from municipal and community sources, for the preservation and treatment of public drinking water supplies, and to minimize the adverse economic, social, health, and aesthetic effects of pollution. This publication is one of the products of that research; a most vital communications link between the researcher and the user community.

The ability of activated carbon to adsorb certain types of organic compounds has frequently been demonstrated. In this publication the results of research on the application of activated carbon to reduce the levels of organic contaminants in drinking water is examined.

Francis T. Mayo, Director
Municipal Environmental Research
Laboratory

ABSTRACT

This research program was conducted to determine how effectively humic substances and the trace contaminants 2-methylisoborneol, geosmin, the chlorophenols and polynuclear aromatic hydrocarbons were adsorbed by activated carbon under the competitive adsorption conditions encountered in natural waters. Data were collected using isotherm tests and small-scale laboratory columns.

Humic substances were obtained from a commercial source, a well water, leaf extract, and soil extract, and some of the materials were separated into the humic acid and fulvic acid fractions. The molecular weight distributions of the fractions were determined by gel permeation chromatography and ultrafiltration. Significant differences in the adsorbability, haloform formation potential, and fluorescence of the various fractions were observed.

A procedure for easily synthesizing the earthy-musty odor-causing compound 2-methylisoborneol (MIB) was developed, and a gas chromatographic analytical technique for quantitative analysis of MIB and geosmin down to 0.1 µg/l was successfully formulated and tested. Humic substances compete with MIB and geosmin for adsorption sites on activated carbon and significantly reduce its capacity for these compounds. These naturally occurring odorous compounds were found to be much more strongly adsorbed than the humic substances.

Both the chlorophenols and the polynuclear aromatic hydrocarbons are very strongly adsorbed. Strong competition was observed between anionic and neutral species of 2,4-dichlorophenol and 2,4,6-trichlorophenol, even at the 1 µg/l-concentration level. The Langmuir model for competitive adsorption, or the Jain and Snoeyink modification of that model, conformed well to the observed data, with one exception at pH 7.0. The presence of the various humic substances also caused a significant reduction in chlorophenol adsorption capacity. Also, humic acid did not interfere with the rate of adsorption of a model polynuclear aromatic hydrocarbon, anthracene.

This report was submitted in fulfillment of EPA Grant No. R 803473 by the University of Illinois under the sponsorship of the U.S. Environmental Protection Agency. This report covers the period January 6, 1975, to July 5, 1977, and the work was completed July 5, 1977.

CONTENTS

FIGURES

viii

TABLES

ACKNOWLEDGMENT

The assistance of Dennis Beckmann, Paul Boening, David Dunn, Dennis Herzing, Terry Temperly and Neville Wood in producing material for portions of this report is acknowledged. The adsorbents used in this study were supplied by the manufacturers.

SECTION 1

INTRODUCTION

STATEMENT OF PROBLEM

Odor problems plague the majority of water treatment plants. Granular activated carbon (GAC) beds now are being used in the U.S.A. predominantly for the removal of odor-causing compounds and are reported to be effective for certain types of odors of biological origin for up to 3 to 5 years (Love et al., 1973). Although only limited data have been reported on the use of GAC for removal of odors of predominantly industrial origin (Dostal et al., 1965), bed life may be much reduced. Unfortunately very few data are available to indicate the mechanism of removal and to enable the application of findings at one water treatment plant to odor problems at other locations. It also is not possible to say whether selected trace organics will adsorb similar to the odor compounds or whether they will rapidly saturate the GAC bed thus making thermal regeneration necessary.

Humic substances in water supplies are also of much concern. These materials react with chlorine to produce haloforms (Rook, 1976; Stevens et al., 1976; Symons, 1976), they occupy adsorption sites on the carbon surface thereby reducing the adsorption capacity for selected trace compounds (Herzing et al., 1977), and they associate with metal ions, pesticides, phthalates and possibly other organics (Schnitzer and Khan, 1972). Humic substances constitute the major fraction of organics in most natural waters. There exists little information on the magnitude and nature of the competitive effects of humic substances, or information on how humic materials from various sources can be removed by adsorption. For these reasons humic substances were an important part of this study.

OBJECTIVES

The objectives of this study were to

1. Characterize humic substances from different sources and to determine how these materials are adsorbed and the extent to which they compete with selected trace organics for adsorption sites on activated carbon.

2. Determine how geosmin and 2-methylisoborneol (MIB), causative agents of earthy-musty odor in water supplies, adsorb on carbon at their threshold odor level in the presence and absence of humic substances

1

3. Determine how mixtures of chlorophenols, compounds which are odorous and which are representative of other undesirable compounds, adsorb at the µg/l level in the presence and absence of humic substances. Especially important is the degree to which the presence of one chlorophenolic species causes a reduction in the capacity of carbon for other chlorophenols.

4. Determine whether the adsorption of polynuclear aromatic hydrocarbons, some of which are proven carcinogens, is affected by the presence of humic substances.

Achievement of these objectives will permit an assessment of whether past results on GAC adsorption of odor compounds are generally applicable, and whether selected, important trace compounds will adsorb similar to the odor compounds.

ADSORBATE CHARACTERISTICS AND BACKGROUND INFORMATION

Humic Substances

According to Schnitzer and Khan (1972) humic substances are compounds which are amorphous, brown or black, hydrophilic, acidic, polydispersed substances of molecular weight of several hundred to tens of thousands. In contrast, the nonhumic substances are those such as proteins, carbohydrates, carboxylic acids, etc. which exhibit recognizable chemical characteristics. The humic substances which are found in water can be classified into two broad categories. The first is humic acid which is soluble in dilute alkaline solutions but precipitates in strongly acidic solutions. The second is fulvic acid which is soluble in both acidic and basic solutions.

These fractions are structurally similar but differ in molecular weight, ultimate analysis and functional group content. Both fractions generally are relatively resistant to microbial degradation, form water soluble and insoluble salts and complexes, and interact with clays and organic matter in solution. It appears that the carboxyl, hydroxyl, and carbonyl groups are the predominant functional groups in humic materials and the relative proportions of these are an index of humic substance reactivity (Schnitzer and Khan, 1972). The carbon content of humic acid ranges from 50 to 60 percent, the oxygen from 44 to 50 percent, the nitrogen from 1 to 3 percent, and the sulfur from near 0 to about 2 percent.

Some adsorption studies have been conducted on humic substances, or on fractions of organic matter which include the humic substances. A pilot plant with a 30 in. GAC filter operated at 2 gpm/ft^2 treating raw Ohio River water has been evaluated for elimination of haloform precursors. It was shown that after 3 to 4 weeks of operation, sufficient material was being passed through the bed to produce measurable amounts of chloroform when the effluent was chlorinated, and after 10 weeks the concentration of the GAC bed effluent was about 50% of the concentration formed when GAC was not used (U.S. Environmental Protection Agency, 1975).

Sontheimer and Maier (1972) carried out an extensive evaluation of 10 different commercial carbons to determine their ability to remove organic matter as measured by absorption of UV light at 240 nm. River Rhine water was used which had been filtered through the river bank, (this removes many biodegradable organics and some dilution of river water with ground water takes place), ozonated and filtered. The conclusions which could be drawn from their results were:

1. The relative positions and slopes of the isotherms were dependent upon the point on the lower Rhine where the sample was taken and upon the time of the year and the rate of flow of the river.

2. The phenol number and the BET surface area do not provide a good indication of carbon effectiveness for organic removal by carbons prepared from different raw materials or by different activation processes. However, if the same raw material and the same activation process are used, better adsorption properties are associated with the higher values of these parameters. It is also likely that the more extensively activated carbons will cost more, however.

3. The least effective of the 10 carbons in the past had proven to be very effective for odor removal.

Their results thus provide strong evidence that the adsorbability of this organic matter is dependent on the type of material being adsorbed.

Sontheimer and Maier (1972) further evaluated whether the relative efficiencies of the carbons as indicated by the isotherms could be observed in pilot scale tests using 1 m deep beds. While the results were not entirely conclusive, it was observed that the better carbons based on the isotherm evaluation generally removed more material in the carbon beds. The total amount of adsorbed material as indicated by extraction with dimethyl-formamide after a period of operation yielded results consistent with those obtained by analyzing the column effluent. It was further observed that all of the carbons tested in beds seemed equally effective for odor removal, but that saturation of the carbon's capacity for total organics was reached much before its capacity for odorous compounds was reached. They also found evidence indicating that some of the odor compounds were removed in the upper part of the bed by biological activity.

In later work by Schweer and co-workers (1975), the removal of sulfur containing organics by GAC and other treatment processes was found to parallel TOC removal.

Sontheimer (1974) reports pilot plant data obtained at the waterworks in Düsseldorf showing the efficiency of 3 different carbons for removal of TOC and total chlorinated organic compounds (TOCl) as determined by the technique of Kühn and Sontheimer (1973a, 1973b), as well as specific chlorinated organics. TOCl is a measure primarily of the lipophyllic organic group of compounds. This group of compounds practically never occurs in nature, are difficult to decompose biologically, and are frequently hazardous to health. There are currently two methods used to determine these compounds.

3

The first involves adsorption of them onto carbon or a synthetic resin and then to extract with dioxane or dimethylformamide. The organic chlorine in the extract can then be analyzed by combusting the sample in a quartz combustion tube and then determining the chloride produced by microcoulometry (Kühn and Sontheimer, 1973a). The second involves direct combustion of the carbon sample containing adsorbed organochlorine compounds and determination of the chloride which is produced by either microcoulometry or a chloride ion electrode. Care must be taken to eliminate interference from inorganic chloride adsorbed on the carbon (Kühn and Sontheimer, 1973a, 1973b). The phenol number and surface area were again found to have no relationship to the adsorption efficiency. Also the carbon which adsorbed the most total organic matter from bank filtered and ozonated Rhine River water over a 6 month period of time, as indicated by TOC measurements on the filter influent and effluent as well as by extraction of the carbon with dioxane and dimethylformamide, adsorbed the least TOCl. The efficiencies of adsorption of specific chlorinated organics, hexachlorocyclohexane, bis (2-chloropropyl) ether and hexachlorobutadiene, paralleled the removal of TOCl. These results indicate the importance of knowing the objective for which carbon is to be used prior to selection of the carbon for an application.

Geosmin and 2-Methylisoborneol

The results of using GAC for the removal of odors presumably of biological origin indicate that odor breakthrough occurs much later than breakthrough of organics measured by a more general parameter such as carbon chloroform extract (CCE) or carbon alcohol extract (CAE) (Robeck, 1975). Because most GAC adsorbers are now in use with the objective of removing odors of biological origin, two compounds of biological origin, 2-methylisoborneol (MIB) and geosmin, were chosen for in-depth study. Close examination of the adsorptive behavior of these species should indicate why the bed-life for such compounds is so long and whether other trace compounds are likely to be similarly adsorbed.

Geosmin is produced by some actinomycetes and blue-green algae (Rosen et al., 1970; Gerber and Lechevalier, 1965; Medsker et al., 1968) and MIB has been identified as a product of actinomycetes (Rosen et al., 1970; Medsker et al., 1969). These compounds have been identified as causative agents of the widespread problem of earthy-musty odors in water supplies (Rosen et al., 1970; Medsker et al., 1969; Jenkins, 1973). A survey in 1957 showed that two-thirds of the water treatment plants surveyed described their odor problems as earthy-musty or, similarly, as that of decaying vegetation (Sigworth, 1957). Dice (1976) also reports survey results indicating that odor from actinomycetes is a frequent problem. MIB and geosmin specifically have been found in surface waters with earthy-musty odors in Europe by the Dutch (Piet et al., 1972), and Japan (Kikuchi et al., 1973a, 1973b).

MIB was identified by Medsker et al. (1969). Geosmin was first isolated and named by Gerber and Lechevalier (1965), while Safferman et al. (1967) later isolated an identical compound. Gerber (1967) presented a partial identification of this compound which was substantiated by Medsker et al.

4

(1968). The threshold odor concentrations of geosmin and MIB are about
0.1-0.2 µg/1 (Jenkins, 1973) and their structural representations are shown
below.

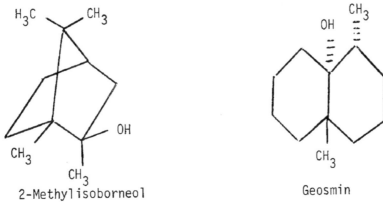

2-Methylisoborneol   Geosmin

Chlorophenols

Chlorophenols were selected as model compounds for our study for a
number of reasons. First, they impart an objectionable taste and odor to
water when present and may have been partly responsible for the reported
chemical tastes and odors in the drinking water that triggered the Lower
Mississippi Study (U.S. Environmental Protection Agency, 1975). In a study
performed to determine the halogenated compounds which result from
chlorinated secondary sewage effluents, trichlorophenol, as well as a number
of other chlorinated aromatic compounds, was found (Glaze and Henderson,
1975). In these two instances, chlorophenols probably were formed by the
reaction of phenols with aqueous chlorine. The primary sources of phenols
in natural waters include natural decay products, waste effluents of coking
plants, brown coal distillery plants, and the pulp and paper industry.
Phenols are used in the synthesis of a number of organic compounds resulting
in their presence in the effluents from many chemical plants. It has been
estimated that the concentration of free phenols in unpolluted streams is
less than 50 µg/1 while that in rivers receiving industrial and municipal
wastewater is frequently greater than 100 µg/1 (Zogorski and Faust, 1974).

According to Burttschell et al. (1959), the chlorination of phenol
proceeds by stepwise substitution of the 2, 4, and 6 positions of the
aromatic ring, in the manner shown in Figure 1. Below each compound in
Figure 1 is listed its threshold odor concentration. The compounds with the
strongest odor-producing potential are 2-chlorophenol, 2,4-dichlorophenol,
and 2,6-dichlorophenol which are detectable at concentrations from 2 to 3
µg/1. These are the compounds primarily responsible for the taste and odor
in water. The 1962 Public Health Service Drinking Water Standards set the
maximum level for total phenols at 1 µg/1 to prevent odor problems. Toxic
effects are thought to occur only at far higher concentrations partly
because phenols are largely detoxified in the mammalian body (McCaull and
Crossland, 1974).

5

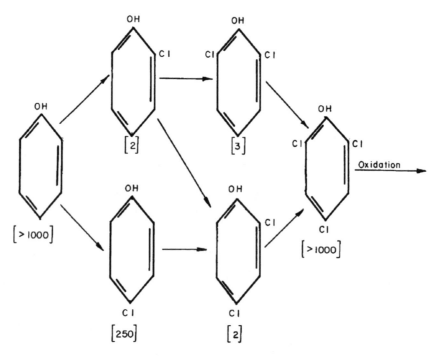

Figure 1. Reaction scheme for the chlorination of phenol.
[ ] indicates odor threshold concentration (µg/l)
(after Burttschell et al., 1959)

The series of reactions leading to the formation and ultimate destruction of chlorophenolic odors involves complex kinetic interrelationships. A short time after mixing chlorine and phenol, eight interdependent reactions are occurring simultaneously. In a study of the kinetics of these reactions by Lee (1967), the expected concentrations of the individual chlorinated phenols were determined as a function of time and other variables. By combining these data with information on the organoleptic properties of the compounds, Lee determined the threshold odor values of chlorinated waters which contained phenols as a function of time, pH, and relative concentrations of chlorine and phenol. Depending on the conditions which existed in the water, Lee observed that different mixtures of chlorophenols may be present at a given time.

The second reason for selecting chlorophenols for use in this study was due to their similarity in structure to a number of pesticides which resist biodegradation. Roughly 25 percent of the pesticides on the world market are compounds which possess a substituted phenol moiety which can be cleaved from the molecule through hydrolysis in natural waters (Friestad et al., 1969). It has been reported that photodecomposition of the herbicide 2,4,5-T (2,4,5-trichlorophenoxyacetic acid) by sunlight in alkaline natural waters may result in the formation of 2,4,5-trichlorophenol and 2,5-dichlorophenol (Crosby and Wong, 1973b). Studies by Crosby and Wong (1973a, 1973b) indicate that this pathway may be general for other commercial phenoxy herbicides. Therefore, the decomposition of pesticides in natural waters may lead to trace amounts of chlorophenols.

In spite of their importance little information is available to indicate how chlorophenols adsorb from waters containing a mixture of chlorophenolic species and humic substances.

Polynuclear Aromatic Hydrocarbons

Polynuclear aromatic hydrocarbons (PAH) are ubiquitous and are found in small but detectable concentrations in air, water and soil samples of all types (McGinnes and Snoeyink, 1974). They are natural products of organic decomposition and are products of incomplete combustion, petrochemical, coal and chemical industrial processes. The concentrations found in water typically range from 0.001 to 10 µg/l and they are concentrated in the food chain because of their favorable solubility in fatty material. Some species of PAH are demonstrated carcinogens at higher concentrations and because of this they are a potential health hazard in water.

Previous studies have shown naphthalene to be very strongly adsorbed from Cincinnati tap water (Robeck, 1975), and that river bank filtration followed by activated carbon treatment removed about 99 percent of PAH from River Rhine water (Andelman, 1973).

In this study, our primary goal was to determine whether PAH associated with humic substances. If this does occur, it is possible that adsorption onto carbon will be controlled by the adsorption characteristics of the humic substances and not by those of the PAH.

APPROACH TO THE STUDY

The study was conducted using aqueous solutions prepared in the labora-tory. Sufficient quantities of the adsorbates were obtained from various sources. MIB was synthesized by us while the geosmin was obtained from the U.S. EPA. The chlorophenols and PAH were obtained from commercial sources. Humic substances were obtained from a commercial source, a local well water, and from leaf and soil extract. Coal-base activated carbon was used as the adsorbent. In most cases it was necessary to develop a quantitative anal-ytical procedure for each of the species.

Small-scale laboratory batch and column tests were used to obtain the desired information on adsorption characteristics. These tests are very flexible and enabled us to look at a wide variety of conditions.

The tests were conducted in such a way so that biological activity did not take place. Short-term tests, and in some cases biocides were used to insure the absence of significant biological growths. It is recognized that biological growths are prevalent in GAC beds at water treatment plants, and that such growths significantly affect the quality of the effluent from these beds (see McCreary and Snoeyink, 1977 for a review) but the scope of this study did not permit us to examine it.

SECTION 2

CONCLUSIONS

Activated carbon adsorbed humic substances in all cases that were studied but the adsorption properties of the substances from different sources varied widely as did the extent to which they competed with selected trace organics for adsorption sites on activated carbon. Humic substances from leaf and soil extract, a well water and a commercial source were examined in detail. Extent of adsorption depended upon solubility, with the less soluble humic acid (HA) fraction being more adsorbable than the fulvic acid (FA) fraction from the same source. The lower molecular weight species from a given FA or HA fraction are more adsorbable than the high molecular weight species presumably because more surface area is accessible to them. The adsorption characteristics of the humic substances are also dependent on the method of analysis used to quantify them. The species which fluoresce the most were found to be the lower molecular weight species and these adsorb best. UV absorbing species did not adsorb as well as those which fluoresce. Solution pH and phosphate concentration also had a marked effect on adsorbability of the humic materials with adsorption generally improving with decreasing pH and increasing phosphate concentration. The haloform formation potential of the humic substances varied widely from source to source, with only one exception, but no dependence on molecular weight was found for fractions of FA or HA. Based on the results of this work it is concluded that when designing an adsorption system to remove haloform precursors or trace organics, it is important that testing be done using the water to be treated to determine design and operating parameters. Because of the variability in adsorption characteristics of the humic substances it would appear that adsorption results obtained at one location will likely not be those obtained at another location.

Concentrations of 2-methylisoborneol (MIB) and geosmin can be quantitatively measured down to 0.1 μg/l by a procedure consisting of extraction, concentration and gas chromatographic analysis with a flame ionization detector. The MIB synthesized from d-camphor was found to be identical to that produced by actinomycetes.

MIB and geosmin are both strongly adsorbed by activated carbon. When present, the humic substances significantly reduce the capacity of carbon for these compounds, more so before equilibrium is achieved than at equilibrium. Commercial HA and the humic substances from well water each had differing competitive effects on MIB. The capacity of carbon for geosmin was reduced to a greater extent than was observed for MIB by commercial HA. The performance of laboratory columns was consistent with the isotherm

9

results. Application of distilled water to a partially saturated carbon bed resulted in almost no elution of MIB indicating that it was strongly adsorbed. Assuming complete saturation of the carbon, no leakage and no biological activity, predicted bed life for reduction of MIB or geosmin from 10 µg/l to its threshold odor level of 0.1 µg/l in a 2-foot deep bed is much greater (several months to years) than for reduction of humic substances from 5 to 1 mg/l (1 to 2 months), for example. When both MIB, or geosmin, and humic substances must be removed, humic substance removal will control the life of the bed. In field installations of granular activated carbon, the possibility that odor compounds are generated, or in some instances degraded, by biological growths within the bed cannot be overlooked.

Chlorophenols are adsorbed very strongly by activated carbon at the µg/l level which is near the threshold odor limit for these compounds. The extent of adsorption of 2,4-dichlorophenol (DCP) and 2,4,6-trichlorophenol (TCP) is a function of pH. The neutral species of these compounds predominate at pH below the pK$_a$ values (7.85 and 6.00, respectively, at 25°C) and are adsorbed more strongly than the anionic species. As the number of chlorine atoms substituted on the phenol increases, the solubility of the neutral species decreases and the adsorbability increases; as substitution increases, the pK$_a$ of the species is lowered, however. When water containing phenol is chlorinated with low levels of chlorine, a mixture of chlorophenols will form and thus the extent of adsorption of one chlorophenol in the presence of another chlorophenol is an important consideration. Significant reductions in adsorption capacity (up to 50 percent) of one chlorophenol was caused by the presence of a second chlorophenol. The Langmuir model for adsorption was found to be inadequate for fitting single solute adsorption data over a broad concentration range. To obtain Langmuir parameters for use in competitive adsorption equations, it was necessary to fit the single solute data with a polynomial equation and to use the polynomial to calculate the Langmuir parameters at the desired concentrations. Competitive adsorption studies between DCP and TCP resulted in verification of the applicability of the Langmuir competitive adsorption equation at pH 5.2, and the Jain and Snoeyink modification of this model at pH 9.1. At pH 7.0, where neutral DCP competes with anionic TCP, neither equation was satisfactory. Evaluation of the competitive effects of commercial HA, soil FA and leaf FA showed that the presence of these materials decreased the capacity of carbon for chlorophenol and that each of the materials competed somewhat differently. However, even in the presence of humic substances and another chlorophenol species, it appears that the adsorption capacity is even greater for chlorophenol than it is for MIB and that bed life for chlorophenol will be greater than for MIB and much greater than for humic substances.

Limited experimentation with the polynuclear aromatic hydrocarbon (PAH) anthracene led to the conclusion that there was no significant association between it and humic substances. Thus it appears that the possibility of PAH passage through carbon beds because of its association with the more poorly adsorbable humic substances is not a cause for concern.

The general conclusion made on the basis of this study is that adsorption characteristics of organic substances which one may wish to remove during water purification are highly variable. Past experience with full-scale carbon beds at water treatment plants, used primarily to remove odor, provides little indication of how humic substances and selected trace organics will be removed, for example. Adsorption tests using the water to be treated should be conducted prior to designing systems to accomplish a specific objective. On the basis of this study it is expected, however, that carbon bed life for removal of typical levels of chlorophenols, MIB and geosmin will be much longer than for humic substances.

SECTION 3

RECOMMENDATIONS

Laboratory and field studies should be initiated to develop simplified procedures for characterizing natural organic matter with respect to adsorbability, competitive effects and tendency to form haloforms when chlorinated. Fluorescence response, UV absorbance, TOC and density of selected functional groups should be related to both haloform formation potential and adsorbability and seasonal variability in type of organics should be taken into account. Research should be conducted on procedures other than adsorption, such as coagulation, which may be effective in removing certain fractions of humic substances and thereby increasing carbon bed life.

Field studies should be undertaken at water treatment plants where granular activated carbon is used and where geosmin or MIB is a problem. Carbon samples taken from several depths within the bed should be extracted and the extract should be analyzed for the odor compound to determine the concentration profile in the bed. Determination of the profile at different times will permit a determination of the rate of movement of the odor compound through the bed and verification of the prediction that bed life should be on the order of several months to years. Biological activity in the bed should also be examined to determine whether it is producing or degrading the odor compound within the bed.

Research should be undertaken to develop reliable small-scale adsorption test procedures to be used on-site to determine the best design parameters and operating conditions to treat a given water. The small-scale test results would necessarily have to be compared with large-scale results and this could best be accomplished at locations where pilot- or full-scale studies are being initiated. If small-scale tests can be used successfully, significant reductions in the time and funds required to obtain necessary design and operation information should be possible.

12

SECTION 4

MATERIALS AND METHODS

ADSORBENTS

Two bituminous coal base activated carbons, Filtrasorb 200 (F-200) and Filtrasorb 400 (F-400) were used for this study. Both carbons were prepared by grinding, sieving to the desired size range (i.e., 40 x 50, 50 x 60, or 60 x 80 U.S. standard mesh), washing, and then drying to a constant weight at 120-140°C. See Calgon Activated Carbon Product Bulletin (1969) for general carbon characteristics.

HUMIC SUBSTANCES

Isolation and Purification

The humic substances used in this study were obtained from a commercial source (Pfaltz and Bauer), and were extracted from leaves and soil. Humic substances in well water obtained from a deep well in the Civil Engineering Building at the University of Illinois were also used. The commercial humic acid was purified using the procedure outlined by Narkis and Rebhun (1975), with some modifications. The material was dissolved in 1.5 percent NaOH, filtered, acidified to pH 1 with HCl to precipitate the humic acid, washed until chloride free and dried at 60 to 65°C. The procedure was later changed to employ centrifugation rather than filtration and freeze-drying concentration instead of oven drying. The purification step did not have a significant effect on the humic acid adsorption isotherm as shown by comparison of isotherms determined before and after the purification step.

Well water from a deep aquifer at the University of Illinois was also used as a source of humic material. Prior to use it was aerated and settled to remove the iron. The well water had a yellowish-brown color and a chemical oxygen demand (COD) (Standard Methods, 1975) of about 10 mg/l. It was also analyzed at the USEPA Municipal Environmental Research Laboratory in Cincinnati and found to have a nonpurgeable total organic carbon (NPTOC) concentration of 3.3-3.6 mg/l.

A continuous upflow column (see Figure 2) was used to extract humic material from leaves and a Finch soil. Eight liters of deionized water was cycled continuously through a bed of leaves acquired from a hardwood forest. Air was bubbled into the holding tank to prevent septicity. The water quickly became discolored and after about two weeks of cycling, the organics

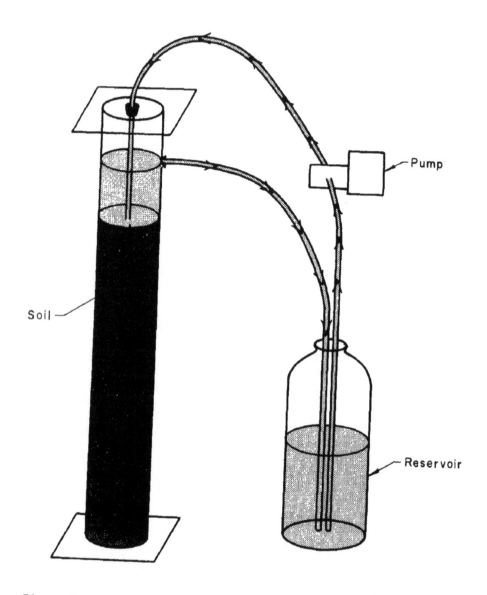

Figure 2. Upflow column for extracting humic material.

which were extracted were concentrated by freeze-drying. The pH of the water was 6.8. Very little material precipitated from the solution at pH 1 indicating that almost no leaf humic acid was present.

Eight liters of a 0.1 M sodium pyrophosphate solution at a pH of 10.6 was cycled through the column with Finch soil. The Finch series is a somewhat poorly drained sandy soil with a strongly cemented subsoil. It was obtained from an area near Traverse City, Michigan. The solution became immediately discolored and contained fine sediment that would not filter readily. After about three days of cycling, the solution was centrifuged in 150 ml polyethylene bottles at 8000 rpm for 30 minutes. This served to deposit the colloidal material. The centrate was then acidified to pH 1 and stirred for approximately one hour. This solution was centrifuged to deposit the precipitated humic acid while the fulvic acid remained in solution.

In order to separate the fulvic acid from the remaining solution, XAD-8 macroreticular resin from Rohm and Haas was used following the procedure of Leenheer and Huffman (1976). The resin was initially washed with methanol and then Soxhlet extracted with ether, acetonitrile, and methanol for 8 hours each. A column 3 cm in diameter and 30 cm long was used for the resin. The XAD-8 resin was followed by a similar bed of XAD-2 resin which resulted in little additional removal (see Figure 3 for typical results).

About one liter of fulvic acid solution at pH 1 was applied to the XAD-8 bed at a flow rate of approximately 2.5 ml/min. This was followed by one liter of 0.1 M NaOH to regenerate the resin. The desorbed fulvic material moved as a band through the bed. Backwashing followed by several bed volumes of deionized water was sufficient to prepare the resin for adsorption of more fulvic acid. The fulvic acid solution obtained from the resin was adjusted to pH 7 and freeze-dried.

Dialysis tubing was used initially to prepare salt-free organics. However, it was observed that the smaller molecular weight organics were passing through the tubing and into the surrounding solution. A similar observation has been reported by Stevenson (1965). Freeze-drying was therefore conducted without prior dialysis.

Molecular Weight (Size) Fractionation

Gel filtration was used for the separation of materials on the basis of molecular weight or size. Gjessing (1976) has shown that the non-excluded fraction from a Sephadex gel column is of questionable value as far as a molecular weight estimate is concerned due to irreversible adsorption inside the gel particle. For the fractionation of humic material he used a series of Sephadex gel columns and selected only the excluded fraction from each column with subsequent concentration and reapplication of the non-excluded fraction to the column with the next smaller molecular weight exclusion limit. We used a similar procedure accompanied by ultrafiltration to obtain our molecular weight fractions.

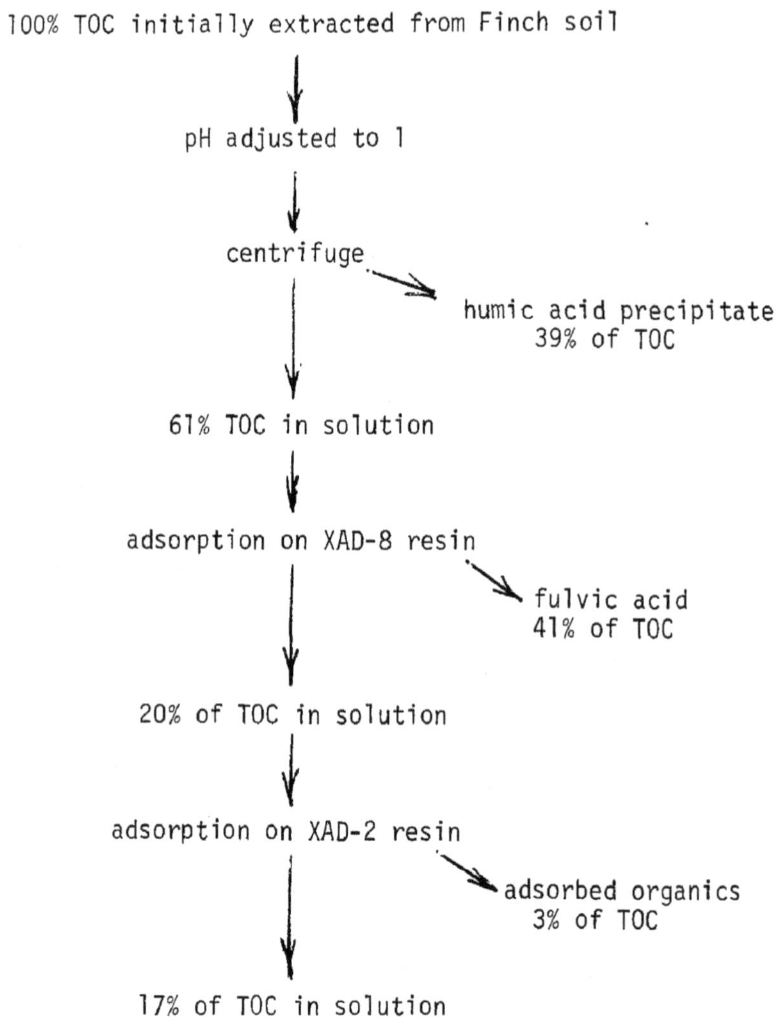

100% TOC initially extracted from Finch soil

↓

pH adjusted to 1

↓

centrifuge ⟶ humic acid precipitate
39% of TOC

↓

61% TOC in solution

↓

adsorption on XAD-8 resin ⟶ fulvic acid
41% of TOC

↓

20% of TOC in solution

↓

adsorption on XAD-2 resin ⟶ adsorbed organics
3% of TOC

↓

17% of TOC in solution

Figure 3. Organic carbon separation from Finch soil monitored by TOC analysis

Table 1 gives the approximate molecular weight exclusion limits for the gels and the molecular weight cut-offs for the ultrafiltration membranes used.

TABLE 1. GEL MOLECULAR WEIGHT EXCLUSION LIMITS AND ULTRAFILTRATION MEMBRANE MOLECULAR WEIGHT CUT-OFF LIMITS

Amicon Diaflo Filters		Sephadex Gels	
UM 10	10,000 MW	G-75	50,000 MW
XM 50	50,000 MW	G-50	10,000 MW
		G-25	5,000 MW
		G-10	700 MW

Our procedure was modified from Gjessing's in that a pH 10, 0.01 M phosphate buffer was used as the eluant to decrease the adsorption of charged groups on the Sephadex particles (Pharmacia, 1974). Also, freeze-drying was used to concentrate the eluted organics rather than roto-evaporation at 40°C.

Each of the gels was boiled in distilled water and allowed to swell for at least the time specified by the manufacturer. The columns were poured through a Buchner funnel fitted on the top of the column with constant stirring and a slow constant flow rate through the column. Finally a glass fiber filter was placed on top of the bed to prevent disturbance when adding sample. The column was thoroughly washed with the phosphate eluant prior to use. Several bed volumes of buffer were required to halt leaching as monitored by TOC. The absence of packing irregularities was confirmed by the application of Blue Dextran dye and analysis of the resulting chromatogram.

One hundred milligrams of organic material dissolved in 2 ml of water was applied to the top of the column. When necessary the solution prepared from the freeze dried organic was filtered to eliminate insoluble residue before application. Irreversible adsorption on the gels was noted when the soil and commercial humic acid were applied and excessive head loss developed with the fine-grade gels. For this reason, only the coarse-grade Sephadex was used for these materials. The volume containing the excluded organics was taken as equal to one bed volume after color appeared in the bed effluent. The first bed volume, consisting of that liquid which passed after application of the sample and before color breakthrough, was discarded. The flow rate was approximately 0.5-1.0 ml/min. Sampling was done with an automatic SMI fraction collector.

To further purify the Sephadex fractions, ultrafiltration was used. As shown in Table 1, the Sephadex G-75 exclusion limit is identical to the molecular weight cut-off for the Amicon XM-50 membrane. The same is true for Sephadex G-50 and the UM-10 filter. The volume containing the excluded organics from the G-75 gel was filtered through the XM-50 membrane. The solution that passed through the membrane was discarded and the organics retained by the filtration unit constituted the purified fraction of molecular weight > 50,000. The XM-50 filter was also used to purify the non-excluded fraction of G-75 by collecting the organics that passed through the filter and discarding those retained by the unit. The filtrate was freeze-dried to small volume and applied to the G-50 gel filtration column. An identical procedure was followed for the G-50 gel and the UM-10 filter. Molecular weight fractions from the other gels were not further purified by ultrafiltration.

A mass balance (see Table 2) was conducted on the Finch soil humic material for the molecular weight fractionation using Sephadex gel filtration. It was observed, as expected, that the humic acid consisted of generally larger weight molecules than the more soluble fulvic acid.

TABLE 2.   FINCH SOIL HUMIC SUBSTANCE FRACTIONATION

Soil Humic Acid		Soil Fulvic Acid	
MW > 50,000	56.4%	MW > 50,000	29%
5,000 < MW < 50,000	32.3%	5,000 < MW < 50,000	48%
MW < 5,000	11.3%	700 < MW < 5,000	20%
		MW < 700	3%

A mass balance was also made on the G-50 gel fractions of Finch soil humic acid using the Amicon XM-50 and UM-10 ultrafiltration membranes. From Table 3 we observe that much of the humic substance excluded from this gel passed through the UM-10 membrane which has the 10,000 MW cut-off. Similarly, much of the volume of < 10,000 MW organics from this gel was retained by the filtration unit. Thus we see that the use of ultrafiltration after Sephadex gel fractionation significantly improves the fractions.

Gjessing (1976), observed the same results and attributed this as a demonstration of the effectiveness of ultrafiltration over gels as a fractionation tool. However, experience in our laboratory demonstrated problems with clogging of the pores of the membrane if prior gel filtration was not used and little difference among the fractions in terms of adsorption capacity when ultrafiltration was used alone as compared with the non-fractionated material. It appears from our results that gel filtration followed by ultrafiltration gives superior results.

TABLE 3. EVALUATION OF G-50 COARSE SEPHADEX FRACTIONS OF SOIL
HUMIC ACID BY ULTRAFILTRATION

Procedure	Molecular Wt.	% of Total	Molecular Wt.	% of Total
Gel Filtration	> 10,000	100	< 10,000	100
Ultrafiltration	> 50,000	42.6	> 10,000	45.4
	> 10,000	14.7	< 10,000	54.6
	< 10,000	42.4		

Fluorescence, UV Absorbance, Total Organic Carbon --

Three primary analytical procedures, ultraviolet absorbance at 240 nm,
fluorescence, and TOC were used for determination of the concentrations of
the humic substances. The fluorescence measurements were made using a
Turner Model 110 fluorometer with an excitation wavelength of 365 nm, an
emission wavelength of 415 nm and a path length of 1 cm. Fluorescence scans
were obtained with an Aminco-Bowman scanning spectrofluorometer. Excitation
spectra and emission scans were obtained for the various humic materials at
identical NVTOC concentrations. The solutions were buffered at pH 7. We
observed that the maximum excitation wavelength was near 360 nm, comparable
to the 365 nm wavelength used on the Turner fluorometer. The maximum
emission peak was very broad and in the range 450-470 nm as compared to the
415 nm wavelength used on the Turner fluorometer. All of the materials had
essentially the same excitation and emission characteristics.

The fluorescence intensity of the unfractionated and fractionated humic
materials at 5 mg/l TOC concentration was found to correlate well with
molecular size (see Table 4). The smaller molecular weight materials were
found to have a much higher fluorescence intensity than the larger molecular
weight substances.

A Beckman ACTA III spectrophotometer was used for the UV measurements.

For well water analysis, the average TOC of 3.45 mg/l of an aerated,
settled sample was used. A standard curve was then prepared by making
dilutions of this sample and determining the UV or fluorescence response of
the dilution. Unknown concentrations were determined by measuring the
fluorescence of a sample and using this standard curve; mass concentrations
are thus based on equivalent TOC and on the assumption that UV absorbance/
unit TOC or fluorescence intensity/unit TOC was the same for the unknown as
for the standard curve samples.

TABLE 4. FLUORESCENCE INTENSITY OF 5 MG/L TOC FRACTIONS
OF HUMIC SUBSTANCES

Sample	Fluorescence Intensity
Commercial Humic Unfractionated	415
Fulvic Soil, Unfractionated	315
Fulvic Soil >50,000	94
Fulvic Soil >5,000	195
Fulvic Soil <5,000	320
Soil Humic, Unfractionated	185
Soil Humic >50,000	57
Soil Humic >10,000	96
Soil Humic <10,000	200
Leaf Fulvic >5,000	237
Leaf Fulvic <5,000	397

Since the soil and leaf humic material was not entirely salt-free, 50 mg/l TOC solutions were prepared. Standard curves were made by making dilutions of these solutions and determining the fluorescence response of the dilutions. Concentrations of unknown solutions could be determined by comparing their fluorescence to this standard curve; mass concentrations are thus based on equivalent TOC and the assumption that the fluorescence intensity/unit TOC was the same for the unknown samples as for the standard curve samples.

Haloform Formation Potential

The haloform formation potential (Stevens and Symons, 1977) of the various humic fractions was determined to further characterize the material. The chloroform analysis procedure reported by Kaiser and Oliver (1976) was modified to suit our needs. All water used for chloroform analysis was distilled in glass followed by exhaustive stripping with N_2 heated over a copper catalyst. This water was then buffered at pH 7 with 0.001 M phosphate. All glassware was thoroughly washed and baked overnight at 450°C before use. Standard chloroform solutions were prepared by injecting chloroform (Mallinckrodt Nanograde) into an appropriate amount of water followed by stirring with minimal headspace overnight. Solutions of the internal standard, 1,1,1-trichloroethane, were prepared in a similar fashion.

Water with chloroform was spiked with a known amount of internal standard solution for analysis. The sample was then placed in a 60 ml separatory funnel with a 2 ml headspace and inverted in a 70° water bath. After equilibration for 45 minutes, about 100 µl of the gas was sampled by gas-tight syringe and injected directly into a Hewlett-Packard gas chromatograph with a Ni^{63} ECD detector. A six foot 0.4% Carbowax 1500 on Carbopack A column was used with argon-methane carrier gas at a flow rate of 36 ml/min. The column was preconditioned at 210°C for one week after packing. Temperature settings were 220°C for the detector, 200°C for the injector port, and 110°C for the column. At these conditions, the retention times for chloroform and 1,1,1-trichloroethane were 2.2 minutes and 3.6 minutes respectively. A typical chromatogram is shown in Figure 4.

Chlorine solutions were prepared by bubbling Cl_2, (Linde high purity gas), into an alkaline solution. The pH was then adjusted to 7 and the solution was stored in a dark bottle at 4°C.

Samples of humic material were prepared at 2.5 mg/l TOC and chlorinated with 10 mg/l chlorine as Cl_2 as measured by the DPD titrimetric method, (Standard Methods, 1975). All water was distilled, stripped, and buffered at pH 7 with 0.001 M phosphate. The reaction solution was mixed and immediately transferred to 125 ml Wheaton Scientific glass vials. Solution was added to fill the bottle without headspace and the caps were crimped over a a Teflon seal. The reaction bottles were placed in an 18°C constant temperature water bath until sampling. At various times the bottles would be reopened and transferred to a second vial containing an appropriate amount of sodium thiosulfate to stop the reaction, crimped again without headspace, and refrigerated until analyzed.

To avoid problems with evolution of chloroform from the standard solutions, the solution was transferred to a series of Wheaton bottles and crimped without headspace. Before each series of separatory funnels was set up, a new bottle of internal standard was removed from the refrigerator and used. After opening and using, the remainder of the solution would be discarded.

It was found that the headspace technique for analysis of chloroform offers distinct advantages over conventional extraction or purge and trap techniques. Several injections could be made from one funnel and the peak height ratios of chloroform to internal standard are reproducible to within 2%. Several funnels could be set up at staggered times to permit considerable time savings over the purge and trap technique. Like the purge and trap technique, only peaks due to volatile species are observed and no problem exists with high retention solvent impurity peaks. Due to the non-linearity of the ECD detector, concentrations above 50 µg/l had to be diluted to a suitable concentration range and the peak ratios had to be compared to a standard curve of several known chloroform concentrations.

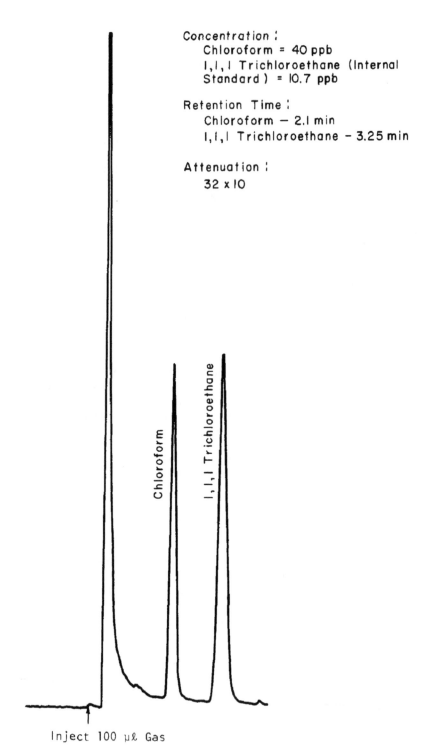

Concentration :
    Chloroform = 40 ppb
    1,1,1 Trichloroethane (Internal
    Standard) = 10.7 ppb

Retention Time :
    Chloroform — 2.1 min
    1,1,1 Trichloroethane — 3.25 min

Attenuation :
    32 x 10

Chloroform

1,1,1 Trichloroethane

Inject 100 µℓ Gas

Figure 4. Typical chloroform chromatogram

2-METHYLISOBORNEOL, SYNTHESIS AND ANALYSIS[1]

The 2-methylisoborneol (MIB) used in this investigation was synthesized from d-camphor, and extraction, concentration, and GC analysis were used to quantify concentrations down to 0.1 µg/l.

Reagents, Solvents and Adsorbents

The reagents, solvents and adsorbents used in the synthesis and analysis are given in Table 5.

TABLE 5. REAGENTS, SOLVENTS AND ADSORBENTS FOR MIB
SYNTHESIS AND ANALYSIS

Substance	Source
d-Camphor, mp 178-180°	Eastman Kodak Company, Rochester, NY
Methyllithium, 1.7 M in ether	Ventron, 8 Congress Street, Beverly, MA
Ether, anhydrous analytical reagent	Mallinckrodt, St. Louis, MO
Hydroxylamine hydrochloride, analytical reagent	Mallinckrodt, St. Louis, MO
Hexane, distilled in glass	Burdick and Jackson Laboratories, Muskegon, MI
Methylene chloride, distilled in glass	Burdick and Jackson Laboratories, Muskegon, MI
Silica Gel, 0.05/0.2 mm, non-activated	Brinkmann Instruments
Florisil, 100-200 mesh, non-activated	Fisher Scientific Supply Co.

Water Samples

The tap water used was that from the Civil Engineering Building, and well water that from a well in the basement. Surface water was that taken from a polluted stream running through the center of Urbana and lake water that taken from a small lake just outside the town.

---

1. Much of the material in this subsection was taken from "2-Methylisoborneol, Improved Synthesis and a Quantitative Gas Chromatographic Method for Trace Concentrations Producing Odor in Water," by N.F. Wood and V.L. Snoeyink, J. Chromatogr., 132, 405 (1977) with the permission of the copyright holder.

Polarimetry

The specific rotation of both natural and synthetic MIB was determined on a Bendix-NPL Automatic Polarimeter which employs the Faraday electro-optic effect to measure optical rotation. To measure the very small rotation observed from the small sample of natural MIB, the instrument had to be operated at high sensitivity. Full-scale deflection of the meter read-out needle to the right or the left then corresponded to a rotation of plus or minus 0.1°, respectively, and rotations could be read to within 0.001°. With 0.1% sucrose the instrument was found to have a calibration factor of 0.952. The 1-cm cell used in this work would not fit the usual cell holder for the instrument, so a cardboard holder was constructed that fitted in the recess in the base of the cell compartment. In this way the cell could be positioned inside the compartment in the same way every time, and a reading from a particular solution could be reproduced exactly.

The specific rotation of the synthetic MIB was also determined using a Carl Zeiss polarimeter.

Thin-Layer Chromatography

Thin-layer chromatography (TLC) was performed on Merck precoated plates of silica gel GOF-254 (0.25 mm). (Stockists may supply the earlier version of these plates from old stocks, but results with these are distinctly inferior in terms of sensitivity and resolution.) Samples were spotted in amounts up to 200 µg. To develop the plates, suitable mixtures of ethyl acetate and hexane were used. Spots were visualized by examination under UV light, treatment with iodine vapor, and by spraying with 1% vanillin in sulfuric acid. Sensitivity with the spray was 1 µg for 2-methylisoborneol, 5 µg for camphor oxime, and 10 µg for camphor. Visualization of camphor spots was quite sensitive to the manner of spraying and sometimes required several hours of standing. Best results with camphor were obtained by a very light spraying followed by a second spraying after 15 minutes. Spray reactions and some typical R_f values are shown in Table 6.

Gas Liquid Chromatography

Gas liquid chromatography (GLC) was performed at 140° on a 183 x 0.2-cm glass column containing Supelcoport (60/80) coated with 3% SP2100 using a F & M instrument (model 810) equipped with a flame ionization detector. The glass column was treated initially with 10% dimethyldichlorosilane in toluene for two hours, washed with methanol, dried, packed with the stationary phase (Supelco, Inc., Bellefonte, PA), and conditioned at 300° for two hours. Flow rates were: nitrogen carrier, 35 ml/min; hydrogen, 30 ml/min; and air 350 ml/min. Injections were made on-column at 270° with a Hamilton 10-µl syringe set at 2-µl with a Chaney adapter. Typical retention times were: camphor, 1.4 min; 2-methylisoborneol, 1.7 min; and camphor oxime, 3.4 min.

TABLE 6. TLC AND MIB AND SOME OTHER CAMPHOR DERIVATIVES

Compound	R_f	Spot formed with 1% vanillin in sulfuric acid
Developing solvent - ethyl acetate:hexane (1:4)		
Camphor Oxime	0.30	Blue-gray. developing slowly
Borneol	0.34	Sharp translucent, developing slowly
Unknown for HBr on 2-methylisoborneol	0.38	Bright crimson developing immediately
Isoborneol	0.41	Yellow-brown, turning blue
2-Methylisoborneol	0.49	Bright crimson, developing immediately
Camphor	0.59	Translucent, developing very slowly

GLC proved invaluable for analyzing and for monitoring the formation of the camphor oxime, the course of liquid-liquid extractions, and the eluants from the silica gel and florisil columns. Before injection, small aliquots of both aqueous and organic solutions were diluted 1:250 with hexane.

Specific Rotation of Natural MIB

Natural MIB investigated in this work originated from Streptomyces sp CWW3 isolated from Lake Michigan. It was contained in a by-product kindly sent to us by the Environmental Protection Agency from the production of geosmin by Dr. Nancy Gerber of Rutgers University for the Agency (Gerber, 1974). The by-product, a dark tar, was found by GLC to contain traces of what were probably olefins (0.6 min and 0.7 min), about 35 mg of geosmin (4.6 min), and only 14.0 mg of 2-methylisoborneol (1.5 min).

The MIB was isolated by liquid chromatography of the by-product on silica gel. Though probably not essential to the operation, advantage was taken of its convenient availability to use modern liquid chromatography equipment. A stainless steel column (60 cm x 0.71 cm id) was packed with silica gel and connected with stainless steel fittings to a Waters pump (model M 6000 A), through a Waters loop injection (model U 6 K). Methylene chloride was pumped through the column at 2 ml/min and the by-product was injected in about 1 ml of the same solvent. Fractions of 10 ml were collected and analyzed without dilution by GLC; results are shown in Table 7. Total

TABLE 7. ISOLATION OF MIB BY COLUMN CHROMATOGRAPHY OF A NATURAL PRODUCT

Adsorbent: silica gel
Eluant: methylene chloride
Fractions: 10 ml

Peak Height by GLC

Fraction	Unknown (r.t. 0.6 min)	Unknown (r.t. 0.7 min)	MIB (r.t. 1.5 min)	Geosmin (r.t. 4.6 min)
2	7.5	9.6		
3	3.4	4.4		
4				15.0
5				48.4
6			5.7	
7			48.4	
8			25.4	
9			4.0	
10			0.1	

1. r.t. = retention time

recovery of MIB was estimated as 14.5 mg. Fractions 7-9, that were homogeneous in 2-methylisoborneol by GLC, were combined and found to be homogeneous by TLC also. Removal of methylene chloride was carried out on a rotary evaporator with the bath temperature at 30° and the evaporation terminated as soon as it appeared that all solvent had been removed. The residue was a clear gum weighing about 17 mg.

The residue was transferred with ethanol to a quartz cell (1 cm x 1 cm id) and made up to a calibration mark of 0.905 ml on the sidearm. The cell was sealed with a Teflon stopper and an air bubble in the sidearm manipulated around the entire cell to produce a homogeneous solution. The observed rotation was -0.023°, and allowing for the ethanol blank of -0.003° and the calibration factor of 0.952, this corresponded to a corrected rotation of -0.019°. The concentration of MIB in the cell solution was found to be 0.0136 g/ml after a 9.8 μl portion had been diluted to 1.0 ml with ethanol and analyzed by GLC.

$$\text{Thus } [\alpha]_{20}^{D} = -\frac{0.019}{0.1 \times 0.0136^{\circ}} = -14^{\circ}$$

Mass Spectrometry

The mass spectrum of MIB was recorded on a Finnigan 3300 quadrupole instrument using the solid probe.

Infrared Spectroscopy

Infrared spectra were recorded on a Beckman IR-20A from samples as potassium bromide pellets (1 mg in 200 mg) or 10% solutions in chloroform.

Evaporations

Analytical extracts of methylene chloride were concentrated using the apparatus shown in Figure 5. The concentration vessels were made from 25-ml round-bottom flasks and are unavailable commercially. Micro Snyder distillation columns (Burke et al., 1966) like the one shown are supplied by Kontes, Inc., Vineland, NJ. The heating bath used consisted of a pan completely filled with water held at 75°C by means of a small hot plate. The cover was a round aluminum plate (0.5 cm x 25 cm diam.) with a small hole in the center fitted with a thermometer and several holes (4 cm in diam.) to accept concentration vessels. The holes held the vessels securely around the midpoint of the bulb and no additional support was necessary.

Extracts were added to concentration vessels together with a small boiling chip. Glass joints were sealed with a thin film of water. After about 5 min. on the water bath, evaporation was complete and the vessel was cooled in a stream of cold tap water or by allowing it to stand at room temperature before removing the Snyder column. The condensate was about 200 μl. Where maximum sensitivity by gas chromatography was desired, this solution was further concentrated to about 20 μl using a rotary evaporator without a heating bath. To avoid solutions of this small volume evaporating to dryness on standing, about 20 μl of ethanol was sometimes added.

Eluates from columns used in the purification of synthetic and natural MIB were evaporated to dryness using a rotary evaporator with a bath temperature at 30°.

Stock Solutions of MIB

The following stock solutions of MIB were prepared:

	μg/ml
A	100
B	10
C	1
D	0.1

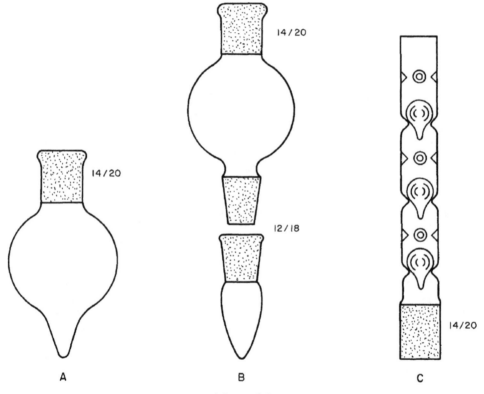

14/20

14/20

12/18

14/20

A   B   C

Figure 5. Concentration apparatus. (A) and (B) are concentration vessels;
(C) is a micro-Snyder distillation column.

A solution was prepared by making 10.00 mg up to 100 ml with ethanol. The other solutions were prepared by successive 1 in 10 dilutions with ethanol. A and B were mixed with similar camphor solutions to form reference mixtures. C and D were used to make additions of MIB to water at 0.1-10 µg/l during recovery experiments.

Stock Solutions of d-Camphor, the Internal Standard

The following stock solutions of d-camphor were prepared:

	µg/ml
A'	80
B'	8
C'	0.8
D'	0.08

Preparation was similar to that described for the MIB solutions.

Reference Mixtures of MIB and d-Camphor

Usually solution A was mixed with A' in the following ratios by volume: 2:1, 1:1, 1:2, 1:5, and 1:10, respectively.

Analytical Method for MIB in Water

An exact volume of internal standard solution was added to 1 liter of the water sample. For an expected MIB concentration of 1-10 µg/l, 5.0 ml of C' was usually used; for 0.1-1 µg/l, 5.0 ml of D' was usually used. The solution was extracted with methylene chloride (1 x 25 ml and 1 x 10 ml) and the extracts run directly into a concentration vessel. Total volume of the combined extracts was 20 ml since about 15 ml of methylene chloride dissolved in the water. After concentration to about 20-200 µl, the extracts were analyzed by gas chromatography using a reference mixture with a similar mixture of MIB to camphor. Peak height ratios were determined by dividing the peak height of the MIB by that of the camphor.

Now assuming response of MIB relative to camphor is constant:

$$h_1 = k \frac{W_1}{w_1}$$

$$h_2 = k \frac{W_2}{w_2}$$

where: h_1 and h_2 are peak height ratios for sample and reference mixture, respectively.

W_1 is the weight of MIB in sample.

29

w_1 is weight of camphor added to sample.

W_2 is weight of MIB per ml of A used to make reference mixture.

w_2 is weight of camphor added to reference mixture per ml of A.

k is a constant

Eliminating k and rearranging:

$$W_1 = \frac{h_1}{h_2} \times \frac{w_1}{w_2} \times W_2$$

$$= \frac{h_1}{h_2} \times \frac{cdv}{cr} \times W_2$$

$$= \frac{h_1}{h_2} \times \frac{dv}{r} \times W_2$$

where: c is the concentration of camphor/ml of A'

d is the dilution factor for the particular stock solution of camphor used with the sample.

v is the number of ml of camphor stock solution added to sample.

r is the ratio of A' to A in the reference solution.

Thus when 5 ml of C' (d = 0.01) was used: 2-methylisoborneol $= \frac{h_1}{h_2} \times \frac{0.01 \times 5}{r}$ x 100 $= \frac{h_1}{h_2} \times \frac{5}{r}$ μg/l.   When 5 ml of D' (d = 0.001) was used: MIB $= \frac{h_1}{h_2} \times \frac{0.001 \times 5}{r}$ x 100 $= \frac{h_1}{h_2} \times \frac{0.5}{r}$ μg/l.

Synthesis of MIB

d-Camphor (60 g) in about 80 ml of ether was added dropwise with magnetic stirring to about 260 ml of 1.7 M methyllithium in ether at such a rate as to maintain the solution under gentle reflux. Before use, the reaction flask was flushed with dry nitrogen fed in through a three-way stopcock in the top of the reflux condenser in one arm and out through the dropping funnel in another arm. Since d-camphor dissolves readily in ether, the solution was prepared in the dropping funnel, so as to avoid exposure of the ether to the atmosphere. After completion of the camphor addition, the solution was refluxed for a further 2 hours and allowed to stand at room temperature overnight. The solution, containing a white precipitate, was then poured onto about 400 g of crushed ice and adjusted to pH 6 with glacial acetic acid. The ether layer was collected by decantation, and the aqueous layer was extracted with more ether (2 x 10 ml). The combined ether solutions were dried over sodium sulfate and evaporated to dryness using a rotary evaporator.

To the residue in 200 ml of ethanol was added 40 g of hydroxylamine hydrochloride in 100 ml of water and 64 g of sodium hydroxide in 100 ml of water to yield two clear layers of approximately equal volume. The solution was refluxed for 8 hours and allowed to stand at room temperature overnight. Water (about 230 ml) was then added with shaking, resulting at first in the formation of a homogeneous solution and finally in the appearance of a slight permanent precipitate. The solution was extracted with hexane (2 x 100 ml) and the combined extracts washed first with 2N sodium hydroxide (15 x 500 ml) and finally with water (2 x 50 ml). The hexane was dried over sodium sulfate and evaporated on a rotary evaporator to yield 24.87 g (37.5%) of MIB as a white crystalline solid.

The product was purified by chromatography on a column of silica gel (6 x 34 cm, 500 g) using methylene chloride as eluant. Eluation of MIB (23.04 g) commenced after 1 liter of eluate had been collected and was complete after 3 liters. Only the first and last 3 g of eluted material showed trace impurities by gas chromatography. The remaining material was homogeneous by both gas and thin-layer chromatography.

The mass spectrum of the product was closely similar to that already published (Medsker et al., 1969) with a parent peak at m/e 168 and a very strong base peak at m/e 95. The infrared spectrum was also closely similar to that published (Medsker et al., 1969). Specific rotation at 20° for the D line using the Carl Zeiss polarimeter was -14.7° (c15.5, ethanol) and using the Bendix polarimeter was -14.9° (c10.76, ethanol) and -3.2° (c10.0, hexane).

GEOSMIN SOURCE AND ANALYSIS

The geosmin was supplied by the U.S. EPA Municipal Environmental Research Laboratory in Cincinnati. Gerber (1974) used Streptomyces sp CWW3 to produce this compound for the EPA. The microorganism was grown at 28°C in a broth medium and the resulting mixture was steam distilled and the distillate extracted with methylene chloride and purified by column and gas chromatography. This species of actinomycetes yielded both MIB and geosmin.

The analytical procedure for determining geosmin concentrations was almost identical to that used for MIB. The only differences were the use of 2-chloronaphthalene as the internal standard and a gas chromatograph column temperature of 140°C.

CHLOROPHENOLS

2,4-Dichlorophenol (2,4-DCP) and 2,4,6-trichlorophenol (2,4,6-TCP) (Eastman Kodak) were used for the chlorophenol studies.

Chlorophenol Analysis

Analysis of chlorophenols was performed on a 5750B Hewlett Packard gas chromatograph equipped with a pulsed Ni[63] electron capture detector. A one-foot coiled glass column packed with 10% DEGS on 80/100 mesh Supelcoport (Supelco, Inc.) was used for the separation of 2,4-DCP and 2,4,6-TCP. The column was conditioned three hours at 200°C with a flow of 20 ml/min carrier gas. Operating conditions were: Column temperature = 170°C, Detector temperature = 230°C, Injection port temperature = 200°C, Carrier gas = dried 5% CH_4-95% Argon at 50 ml/min flow, Pulse interval = 150 µsec. 2,4-Dibromophenol (2,4-DBP) obtained from the Aldrich Chemical Company was selected as the internal standard since it is eluted close to and completely separate from 2,4-DCP and 2,4,6-TCP at these operating conditions; at a given concentration, the detector response is intermediate to these two chloro- phenols; and its physical properties are very similar to the chlorophenols as shown in Table 8.

TABLE 8. CHARACTERISTICS OF THE CHLORO- AND BROMOPHENOLS STUDIED
(Handbook of Chem. & Physics, 1967)

Compound	M.W.	m.p. °C	b.p. °C	Solubility g/100 ml H_2O	pK_a
2,4-DCP	163.01	45	210	0.46	7.85
2,4,6-TCP	197.46	68	244.5	0.08	6.00
2,4-DBP	251.92	40	238.9	0.19	7.30

Nanograde toluene (Mallinckrodt) was chosen as the solvent for sample preparation, for GC analysis, and for extraction of the chlorophenols from aqueous solution for several reasons: the solvent peak does not overlap with any of the peaks of interest nor are there any interfering impurities; it is practically immiscible with water; and the partition coefficients for extraction of chlorophenols from water are high enough to indicate adequate recovery (Korenman, 1974).

Stock standard solutions containing 1 µg/µl 2,4-DBP and another containing 1 µg/µl of both 2,4-DCP and 2,4,6-TCP were prepared as outlined by the U.S. EPA (1971) for organic pesticides. Working standards were prepared from the stock solution using a micro-syringe and then stored at

5°C. A typical working curve for 2,4-DCP is shown in Figure 6. Ratios of the peak heights of the chlorophenols to that of 75 µg/l 2,4-DBP were computed and plotted versus chlorophenol concentration. The chromatogram in Figure 7 showing 80 µg/l of both 2,4-DCP and 2,4,6-TCP and 75 µg/l 2,4-DBP is typical of the data used to obtain the curves. Day-to-day variation in detector response and column performance was significant enough that standard curves had to be prepared prior to each set of chromatographic analyses.

Extractions were performed using 100 ml of the adsorbate solutions adjusted to pH 2.0 to ensure that the less soluble neutral species were present. When the chlorophenol concentration was high, dilutions were prepared to ensure peak heights fell on the standard curves. Prior to extraction, 7.5 µl of 50 mg/l 2,4-DBP in distilled water was added to the solution. Extractions were performed in 250 ml separatory funnels with 5 ml toluene resulting in a concentrating factor of 20X. The solutions were shaken for five minutes as recommended by Korenman (1974), and 30 minutes were allowed for complete separation of the phases. Recoveries of the chlorophenols relative to 2,4-DBP were found to be 100 percent for 2,4-DCP and 104 percent for 2,4,6-TCP in the concentration range studies. For this procedure the estimated sensitivity limits for 2,4-DCP and 2,4,6-TCP were found to be 1 µg/l and 0.01 µg/l in water, respectively.

POLYNUCLEAR AROMATIC HYDROCARBONS

Various methods were evaluated to determine the concentration of the polynuclear aromatic hydrocarbons (PAH), anthracene (Aldrich) and benzanthracene (Eastman). A fluorometer (Turner Model 110) produced a linear response with concentration. This procedure was satisfactory for pure solutions of PAH, but in the presence of humic substances which fluoresce, the contribution to fluorescence by PAH alone would be impossible to determine. Early attempts were made to extract the PAH from humic acid solution with toluene and to measure the fluorescence of the extract. Some of the humic material was also extracted, however, and good results using fluorescence were not obtained. When the aqueous solution was made basic to a pH of 11, less material was extracted into the organic phase. It was also found that UV absorbance did not offer adequate sensitivity; a 5 cm path length cell was satisfactory for the determination of 20 µg/l of benzanthracene as a lower limit, for example.

Gas chromatography was chosen for the analytical determination of PAH in solution with humic acid. The solution was extracted with cyclohexane (Mallinckrodt) after being made alkaline with several drops of concentrated NaOH to minimize the extraction of humic substances. Cyclohexane was used because it tended to produce less of an emulsion. The SP-2100 column used for the quantitation of MIB and geosmin was found to be suitable for the PAH work. A variety of internal standards was checked, among them carbazole, phenanthrene, fluorene, fluoranthene, 2-methyl naphthalene, 9-methyl anthracene and trans-stilbene. Fluoranthene eluted between anthracene and benzanthracene and thus showed promise as an internal standard if competitive experiments between these two PAH compounds were performed. Fluorene was masked by the solvent front and carbazole and phenanthrene eluted too close

33

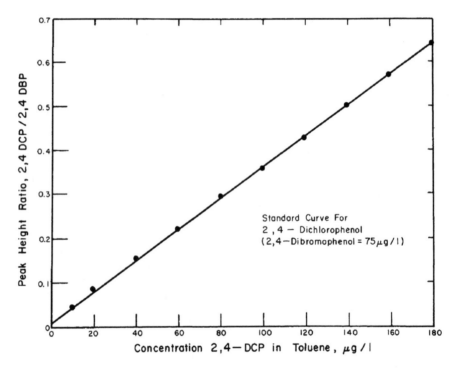

Figure 6. Standard curve for 2,4-dichlorophenol.

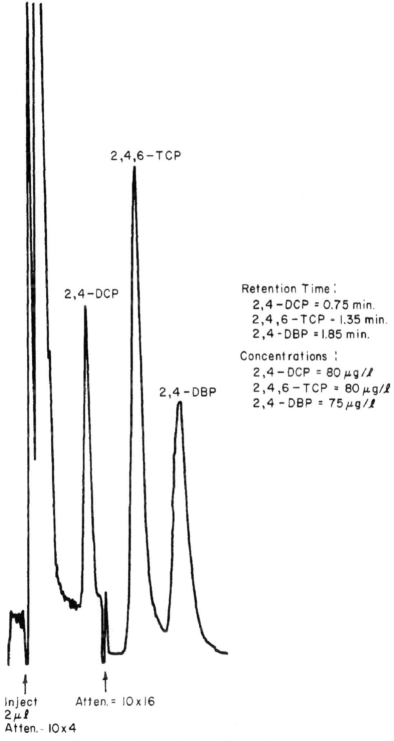

2,4,6-TCP

2,4-DCP

Retention Time :
  2,4-DCP = 0.75 min.
  2,4,6-TCP - 1.35 min.
  2,4-DBP = 1.85 min.

Concentrations :
  2,4-DCP = 80 μg/ℓ
  2,4,6-TCP = 80 μg/ℓ
  2,4-DBP = 75 μg/ℓ

2,4-DBP

Inject
2 $\mu\ell$
Atten.- 10x4

Atten. = 10x16

Figure 7. Typical chlorophenol chromatogram.

to the anthracene peak. Trans-stilbene eluted after the solvent peak and before anthracene and was a logical choice. A portion of it was lost during evaporation, however, possibly due to partial isomerization to the cis-isomer. 9-Methyl anthracene (Aldrich) which eluted after the anthracene was used instead. Tests were performed with standard solutions and it was found that extraction of a 75 ml sample successively with 10 ml, 5 ml and 5 ml volumes of cyclohexane removed 99 percent of anthracene from solution. It was also shown that removal of solvent with the micro Kuderna-Danish (K-D) evaporator resulted in no absolute losses of PAH.

A 6 foot, 3 percent SP-2100 (Supelco) column was used with a nitrogen carrier gas at a flow rate of 40 ml/min. The temperature settings were 210° for the column, 260° for the injector, and 280° for the detector. At these conditions, retention times for the anthracene and methyl-anthracene were 1.9 minutes and 2.5 minutes, respectively, as shown in Figure 8.

Solutions of anthracene to be analyzed were made alkaline to pH of 11 and extracted with three volumes of cyclohexane. The cyclohexane phases were combined and spiked with a known amount of internal standard. This was then concentrated to about 200 µl in a micro K-D evaporator. If further concentration was necessary it was done on a rotary evaporator without a heating bath similar to the MIB analytical procedure.

ADSORPTION TEST PROCEDURES

Isotherm Tests

Humic Substances --

The tests were conducted by adding an accurately weighed dose of carbon to a series of 250 ml bottles containing solution of known concentration. The solution volume was 150 ml. The bottles were placed on a shaker for 4-7 days at room temperature, after which time the equilibrium solution concentration was determined. Several identical samples were analyzed daily to verify that equilibrium was achieved.

A buffer was not used for nonfractionated commercial humic acid or well water, but it was necessary to use it for those humic substances which were fractionated using a phosphate eluant. In order to prepare a phosphate buffered solution at a fixed concentration of phosphate when the organics also contain phosphate, the Vanadomolybdophosphoric Acid test was employed to determine the proper amount of phosphate to add (Standard Methods, 1975). The phosphate concentration of the solution containing only the organics was measured and the additional required phosphate was then added. Equilibrium concentrations were determined by fluorescence or, in some cases, UV absorbance.

MIB and Geosmin --

Stock MIB and geosmin solutions were made by dissolving the compound in ethanol and then diluting with deionized distilled water. The desired

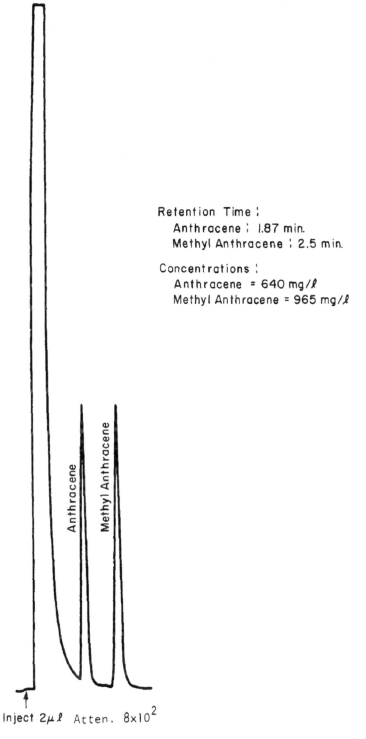

Retention Time :
  Anthracene : 1.87 min.
  Methyl Anthracene : 2.5 min.

Concentrations :
  Anthracene = 640 mg/ℓ
  Methyl Anthracene = 965 mg/ℓ

Anthracene

Methyl Anthracene

Inject 2μℓ Atten. 8x10^2

Figure 8. Typical anthracene chromatogram.

37

quantity of solution was prepared in this manner immediately before starting
the tests. MIB is very stable in ethanol and the ethanol thus introduced
into the adsorption test systems, on the order of 1 to 5 mg/l, had no notice-
able effect on the isotherms as shown by comparing isotherms prepared using
different ethanol concentrations, consistent with its poor adsorption characteristics.

Most of the batch data for MIB and geosmin were obtained using 1 liter
samples in 2-1/2 liter cylindrical bottles. The tests were generally conducted by setting up a series of bottles each with the same concentration of
adsorbate but with different doses of carbon. Blanks were also used which
contained no carbon. It was determined that 8-9 days were necessary for
equilibration at the μg/l concentration level on the gyratory shaker while
only 4-5 days were required when there was more vigorous shaking on a
reciprocating shaker or if the bottles were tilted about 30° from the
horizontal on the gyratory shaker. Other tests were conducted by putting a
large dose of carbon into a single bottle with a high concentration of
adsorbate. After equilibration, the solution was decanted and another
solution containing adsorbate was contacted with the carbon and the sample
was then re-equilibrated. This process was repeated several times to
establish an adsorption isotherm.

A considerable amount of data were gathered for MIB using a procedure
which did not result in equilibrium. Some of these data are presented in
this paper because they are important when carbon is used under nonequi-
librium conditions.

Chlorophenols --

Chlorophenol stock solutions were prepared just prior to use by dissolving a known amount of compound in distilled water adjusted to about pH 9
with NaOH to ensure that the compound was dissolved. 2,4-DCP and 2,4,6-TCP
are weak acids and were studied in both their dissociated and undissociated
forms. To ensure the predominance of either the neutral or anionic form,
the pH of the solution was adjusted to at least one unit below or above the
compound's pK_a value (Ward and Getzen, 1970). The solutions were buffered
with 10^{-2} M phosphate salts. A series of 2-1/2 liter bottles were filled
with one liter of the adsorbate solution. Amounts of Filtrasorb 400 carbon
were added to each bottle to yield the desired equilibrium concentration
with at least two bottles containing no carbon to serve as blanks. The
bottles were sealed with Teflon-lined caps and placed on a model G10 gyratory shaker (New Brunswick Scientific) operated at 200 rpm. The shaker
compartments were angled to ensure adequate mixing. At least 12 days were
allowed for equilibration. All studies were performed at room temperature
which varied ±2°C. Prior to extraction and analysis, the solutions were
filtered through fiberglass filters to eliminate carbon fines. Studies were
performed which indicated that chlorophenols did not adsorb on the filter.

Column Tests

MIB and geosmin breakthrough curves were developed using continuous
flow column systems and deionized water. Two grams of 40 x 50 mesh carbon
(unless stated) were placed in 1.27 cm diameter columns. In some cases, the

carbon was sandwiched between several cm of sand, also of 40 x 50 mesh size, although this had little effect on column performance. Bed depth was 2.7 cm and empty bed contact time was on the order of 0.1 minute. The flow rate of 2 liter/hr (6.5 gpm·ft^2) was kept constant by use of a metering pump. The tests were conducted at room temperature of approximately 23°C. Samples were collected on a regular basis and then analyzed to obtain a record of effluent concentration vs. time.

SECTION 5

RESULTS AND DISCUSSION

HALOFORM FORMATION POTENTIAL OF THE HUMIC SUBSTANCES

The haloform formation potential of the humic substances used in this study was determined to further characterize these materials. In Figure 9 chloroform formation with time by the various humic substances is shown. It is interesting to note that not all humic materials will produce the same amount of chloroform per unit weight of TOC. The yield of chloroform from the soil humic acid is lower than from the soil fulvic acid while soil fulvic acid and leaf fulvic acid give nearly the same result. The large difference between commercial humic acid and soil humic acid illustrates that the source of the material is important.

In Figure 10 we observe that various molecular weight fractions of soil fulvic acid yield about the same amount of chloroform as the unfractionated soil fulvic acid. This would seem to indicate that molecular weight fractions have the same density of those functional groups which produce chloroform as the unfractionated group of compounds. In Figure 11, similar results are shown for soil humic acid fractions. The differences between the curves are not considered significant.

Another experiment was performed to evaluate the removal of haloform precursor by activated carbon. One liter of 5 mg/l TOC commercial humic acid was equilibrated with an amount of activated carbon to give about 50 percent removal as indicated by fluorescence. After one week the blank solution was diluted to give an identical fluorescence reading as the equilibrated solution and both were chlorinated using the above procedure. After 8 hours, the chloroform concentration of the diluted blank was 115 μg/l. The chloroform yield of the carbon equilibrated solution was 198 μg/l, a 72 percent increase over the blank. Because it has been shown that the various molecular weight fractions have the same haloform formation potential as the unfractionated material, this finding is consistent with our adsorption results which show that carbon preferentially removes the low molecular weight compounds which are also the most highly fluorescent. Thus the decrease in fluorescence is not matched by an equal decrease in chloroform formation and is not matched by an equal decrease in TOC.

ADSORPTION OF HUMIC SUBSTANCES

The results of batch studies using commercial humic acid are shown in Figure 12. The data are based on analysis by fluorescence and UV absorbance,

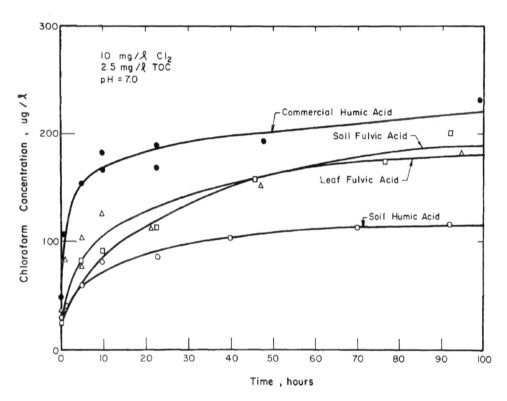

Figure 9. Chloroform formation from humic and fulvic acids.

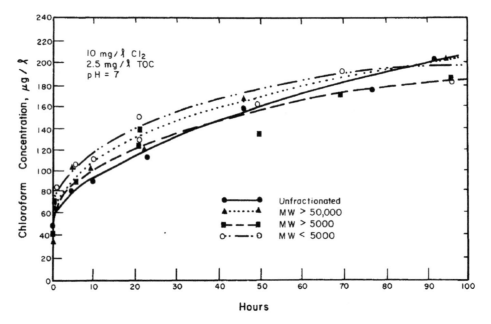

Figure 10. Chloroform formation from soil fulvic acid.

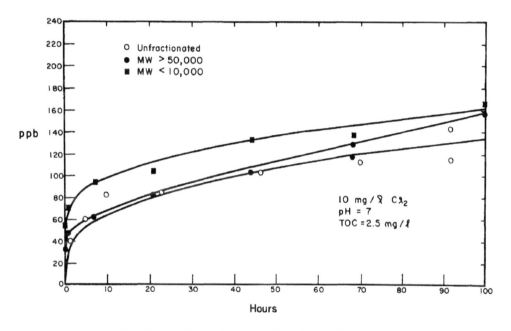

Figure 11. Chloroform formation from soil humic acid.

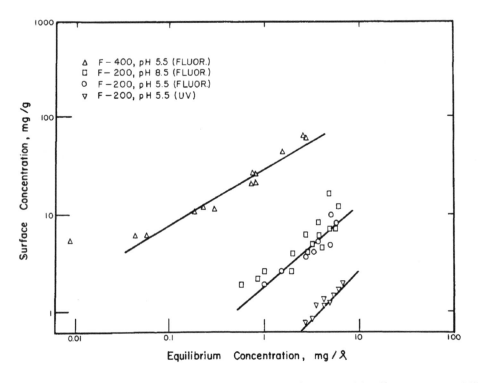

Figure 12. Adsorption isotherms for commercial humic acid measured by fluorescence and UV.

as indicated. F-400, which has a larger average pore size and about 200 m^2/g more surface area than F-200, showed a much higher capacity for humic acid. The data show no difference in the adsorption isotherm using F-200 as the pH is changed from 5.5 to 8.5, however. The analytical technique used to determine humic acid concentrations is shown to have a very significant effect on the results. The material which absorbs UV light adsorbs less strongly than the material which fluoresces.

Figure 13 shows data for adsorption of organic matter on F-200 from well water compared to the isotherm for commercial humic acid reproduced from Figure 12. There appears to be no significant effect of pH on adsorption of humic material from the well water. There is also more fluorescent organic matter removed per gram of carbon from well water than from the commercial humic acid solution. Based upon our results presented earlier which showed lower molecular weight material to fluoresce more and be adsorbed to a greater degree, the presence of a greater number of low molecular weight compounds is indicated. However, this remains to be demonstrated

Figure 14 demonstrates the effect of phosphate buffer concentrations on the soil fulvic acid adsorption at pH 7. The higher buffer concentrations yield higher capacities, the specific reason for which is not apparent.

Figure 15 demonstrates the effect of pH on soil fulvic acid adsorption in the presence of 0.001 M phosphate buffer. Due to the acidic character of the natural organics, a decrease in pH renders them less soluble and thus more readily adsorbed on activated carbon. This rather significant effect is in contrast to the absence of a pH effect in the pH 5 to 8.5 range reported previously for commercial and well water humic substances. A pH of 7 was chosen for all subsequent isotherms.

Figure 16 compares the adsorption of the various humic materials on F-400. It is interesting to note the different capacities. The soil humic acid adsorbs better than the soil fulvic acid due to its lower solubility in water. This cannot be generalized to all fulvic and humic material, however, as the leaf fulvic acid was adsorbed best of all. It should be able to penetrate smaller pores that are inaccessible to the humic acid molecules.

Figures 17, 18 and 19 show the extent of adsorption of various molecular weight fractions on adsorption capacity. In all cases we observe a steady decrease in extent of adsorption as the molecular weight of the material increases. This probably is due to the inability of the large molecules to enter the smaller pores of the carbon.

45

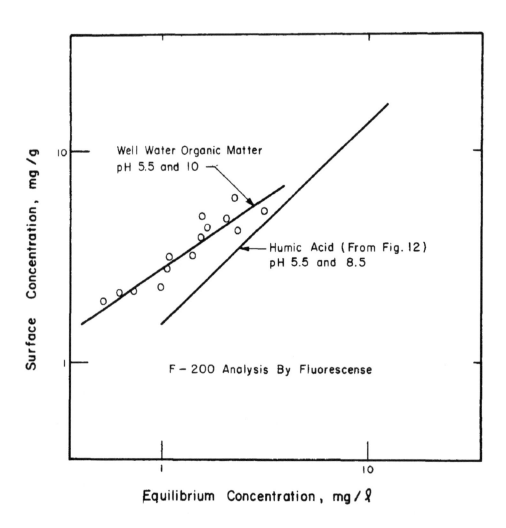

Figure 13. Adsorption of well water organic matter.

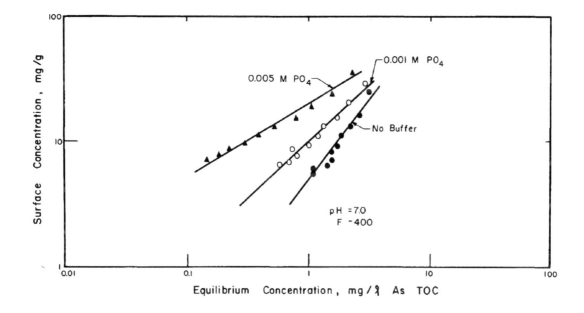

Figure 14.   Effect of phosphate buffer concentration on adsorption of soil fulvic acid.

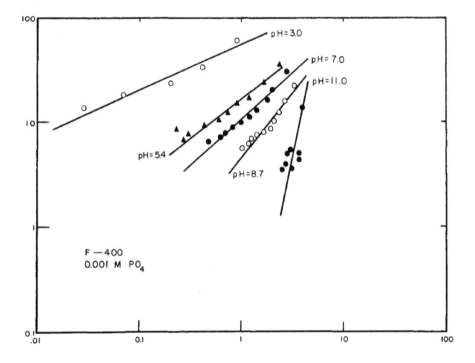

Figure 15. Effect of pH on the adsorption of soil fulvic acid.

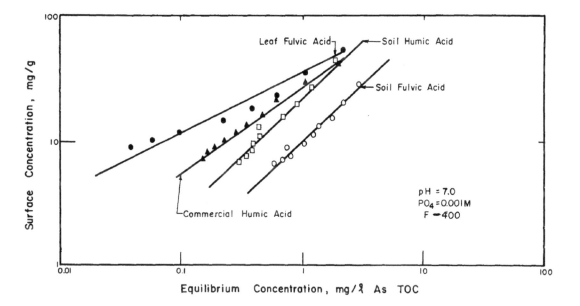

Figure 16. Adsorption of various types of humic substances.

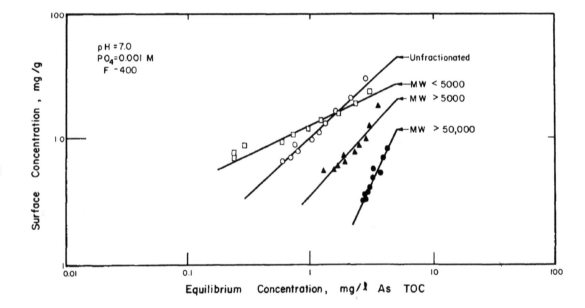

Figure 17. Adsorption of molecular weight fractions of soil fulvic acid.

50

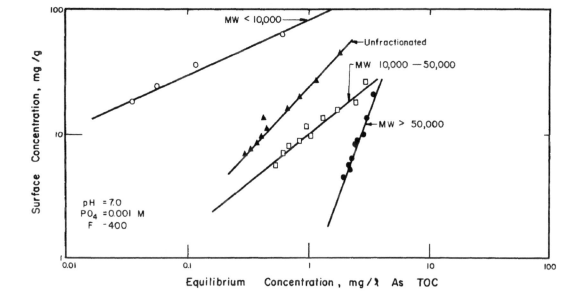

Figure 18. Adsorption of molecular weight fractions of soil humic acid.

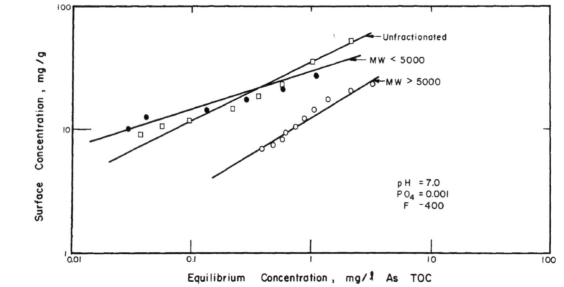

Figure 19. Adsorption of molecular weight fractions of leaf fulvic acid.

MIB SYNTHESIS AND ANALYSIS[1]

Enantiomeric Form of Natural 2-Methylisoborneol

MIB can exist in two optically-active forms with the current Chemical Abstracts names of (1-R-exo)- and (1-S-exo)- 1,2,7,7-tetramethylbicyclo [2.2.1] heptan-2-ol as shown in Figure 20 (Personal communication from D. Weisgerber, Chemical Abstracts Service, 1976). These are derived from d- and l-camphor, respectively (Figure 20). In the literature natural MIB has always been depicted as the S form, although no evidence for this has ever been reported. Since we were interested in studying not only the adsorption of the natural form on carbon beds but also in examining for any concurrent biological activity, we needed to determine which of the two forms occurred naturally so as to synthesize the appropriate one for our experiments.

Accordingly, we have measured the specific rotation of a natural sample of MIB and so determined its enantiomeric form. We isolated the sample by liquid chromatography on silica gel of a product obtained by Dr. Nancy Gerber of Rutgers University from the culture of Streptomyces sp. CWW3 (Gerber, 1974), for the U.S. EPA and supplied to us by the U.S. EPA Municipal Environmental Research Laboratory. The product was mostly geosmin and only 14 mg of pure MIB was obtained. By measuring the optical rotation in ethanol to within 0.001°, a specific rotation of -14° was obtained, in good agreement with the -14.8° reported in the literature (Malkonen, 1964) for MIB obtained from d-camphor. Thus natural MIB exists in the R form.

Synthesis of 2-Methylisoborneol from d-Camphor

Since the first preparation was reported in 1901 (Zelinsky, 1901) MIB has been prepared many times by the action of methylmagnesium halides or methyllithium on camphor (Medsker et al., 1969; Rosen et al., 1970; Malkonen, 1964; Capmau et al., 1968; Fieser and Ourisson, 1953; Zeiss and Pease, 1956). The difficulty with this seemingly easy preparation is that much of the camphor reacts to form an enolate and during the work-up this reverts to camphor, which until now has been difficult to eliminate from the product.

Direct separation of the MIB from the camphor by chromatography has been reported. Liquid chromatography on alumina (Malkonen, 1964; Capmau et al., 1968) has been used, though it is apparently difficult to eliminate the camphor entirely (R. G. Webb and N. N. Gerber, personal communications, 1976). Preparative gas liquid chromatography (Medsker et al., 1969; R. G. Webb and N. N. Gerber, personal communications, 1976) apparently yields a pure product but is limited to the preparation of milligram quantities.

Another approach (Malkonen, 1964) to the problem has been to repeatedly

---

1. Much of the material in this subsection was taken from "2-Methyliso-borneol, Improved Synthesis and a Quantitative Gas Chromatographic Method for Trace Concentrations Producing Odor in Water," by N. F. Wood and V. L. Snoeyink, Jour. Chromatogr. 132, 405 (1977), with the permission of the copyright owner.

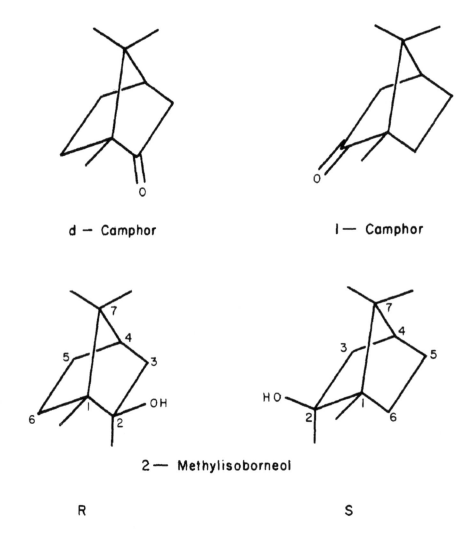

d — Camphor   l — Camphor

2— Methylisoborneol

R   S

Figure 20. Stereochemical structures of 2-methylisoborneol and
camphor enantiomers.

54

treat the crude product with more reagent until the camphor is reduced to such a small proportion that it can be eliminated by recrystallization.

Finally, MIB has been separated from the camphor through its chromate ester (Fieser and Ourisson, 1953; Zeiss and Pease, 1956). Although reduction of the ester with hypophosphorous acid or saponification yielded impure MIB (Fieser and Ourisson, 1953), reduction with lithium aluminum hydride on a small scale appeared to yield pure material (Zeiss and Pease, 1956).

In our synthesis of MIB we chose methyllithium as reagent rather than a methylmagnesium halide, partly because this was conveniently available commercially, and partly because we hoped it would give the higher yield. Figure 21 shows the gas chromatogram from the crude product obtained from 60 g of camphor and 1.3 equivalents of methyllithium after reaction at reflux for 2 hours and overnight at room temperature. Since the response of MIB relative to camphor was 0.90, the observed peak height ratio of 0.50 corresponds to 67 percent of unchanged camphor. When the amount of reagent was increased to 2.0 equivalents, the observed peak height ratio increased to 0.56 corresponding to only a slightly decreased amount of 64 percent of unchanged camphor. Decreasing the reaction time to 2 hours without reflux had no effect on the amount of unchanged camphor. Malkonen (1964) has reported only 37 percent of unchanged camphor using 3.0 equivalents of methylmagnesium iodide. Thus, although the Grignard reagents may not be as convenient to use as methyllithium, they appear to give better yields of MIB.

To eliminate the large amount of camphor in our crude product we decided to selectively react the camphor quantitatively to form a derivative that would be more easily separated than the camphor itself. Many reagents were tested but most were unsuitable because of the particularly unreactive nature of camphor. The exception was alkaline hydroxylamine at reflux. Using the reaction conditions of Lenz (1911) and monitoring the reaction mixture by gas chromatography, it was found that 19 percent camphor remained after 2 hours but reaction to the oxime was complete after 7 hours. A chromatogram of the reaction product is shown in Figure 22.

With the camphor in the form of the oxime it was rather easily eliminated by taking advantage of its acidic properties. First the alkaline reaction solution was diluted with water and extracted twice with a small proportion of hexane. Gas chromatography on the residual solution (Figure 23) and the combined extracts (Figure 24) showed that less than 50 percent of the oxime and more than 98 percent of MIB was in the extracts. Finally repeated washing of the extracts with aqueous sodium hydroxide gradually removed all of the oxime without loss of MIB. The product was essentially pure by gas chromatography (Figure 25).

In another experiment the reaction solution containing the oxime was not diluted with water as above but extracted directly with hexane. Partitioning into the hexane layer was reduced but selectivity improved. Four extractions removed a total of 92 percent of the MIB and only 20 percent of the oxime from the reaction solution, so that complete elimination of the oxime was achieved with far fewer washings of aqueous sodium hydroxide.

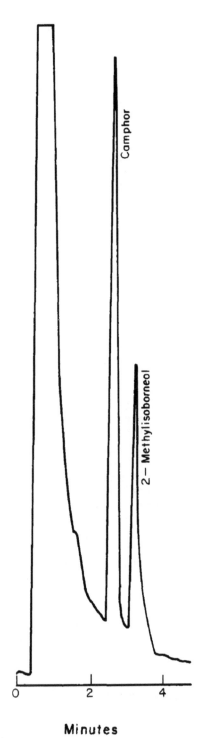

Minutes

Figure 21.   Chromatogram from the product of the action of
methyllithium on d-camphor.

56

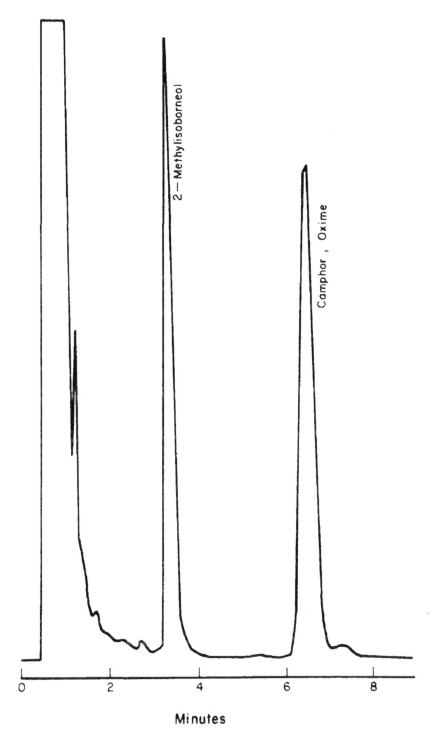

Figure 22.   Chromatogram from the product of the action of methyllithium on d-camphor after treatment with alkaline hydroxylamine.

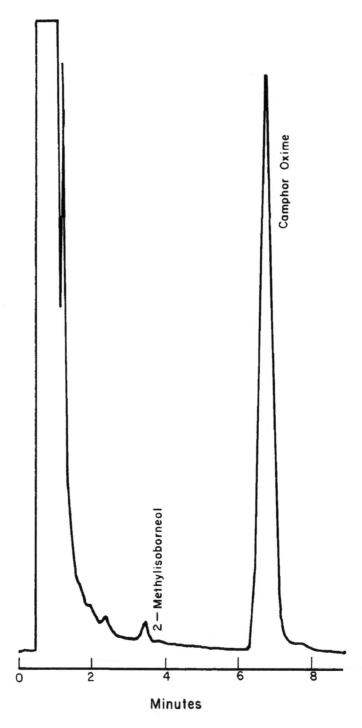

Figure 23. Chromatogram from the residual aqueous solution from the hydroxylamine reaction after hexane extraction.

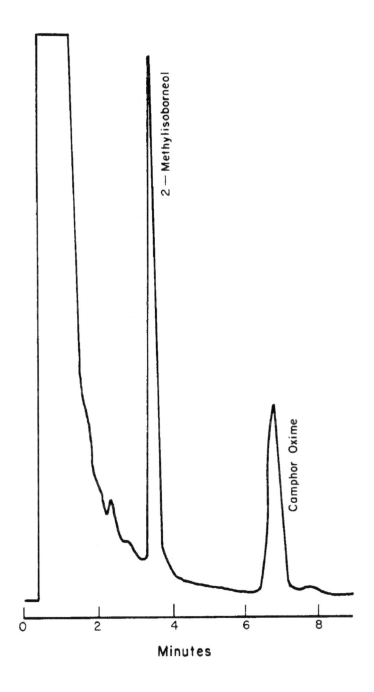

Figure 24. Chromatogram from the hexane extract after the
hydroxylamine reaction.

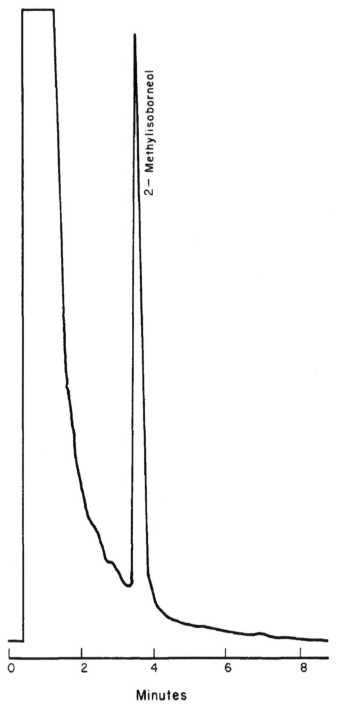

Figure 25. Chromatogram from the hexane extract in Figure 24 after exhaustive washing with 2 N sodium hydroxide.

Thin-layer chromatography in addition to gas chromatography was used to monitor the above work. Table 6 gives details for MIB and related camphor derivatives. Note that the bright crimson color reaction of MIB is quite characteristic and develops immediately with a sensitivity of less than 1 µg. Unfortunately camphor gives only an uncharacteristic translucent spot that develops erratically over a long period with a sensitivity of 10 µg at best. (Other sprays for camphor give even poorer sensitivities [Stahl, 1969].) Camphor oxime does give a characteristic color reaction but this develops only slowly and again with a sensitivity of 10 µg. Despite the limitations with camphor and its oxime, thin-layer chromatography was useful in that it detected impurities in the MIB not revealed by gas chromatography, and thus indicated the need for final purification of the product by liquid chromatography.

Liquid chromatography on alumina has usually been used for the purification of MIB, but our attempt to use basic aluminum oxide (Woelm) led to complete decomposition. This also occurred when an old preparative column of silica gel was used. Even on Florisil there appeared to be slight decomposition as elution was delayed for 10 hours. This was evidenced by the appearance of several very slow developing translucent spots on thin-layer chromatograms of the product. However, MIB homogeneous by thin-layer chromatography was obtained by chromatographing on fresh silica gel and eluting with methylene chloride within 2 hours.

Attempted Preparation of Electron-Capturing Derivatives from 2-Methylisoborneol

Since we were interested in analyzing aqueous solutions of MIB down to 0.1 µg/l by gas chromatography, the use of the sensitive electron-capture detector seemed appropriate. Accordingly, attempts were made to prepare a suitably electron-capturing ester.

Heptafluorobutyric anhydride alone did not react significantly with MIB at room temperature, and even at 60°, 12 hours was required before most of the MIB had reacted. The product was a mixture of two substances whose retention times by gas chromatography relative to that of MIB (0.56 and 0.60) indicated that they were olefins. In benzene in the presence of triethylamine at room temperature, reaction was virtually complete in 1 hour but a similar product resulted. Thin-layer chromatography showed only one major spot (R_f 0.94), which had a bright crimson appearance. After 24 hours the initially predominant substance (relative retention time 0.60) appeared to have partially converted to the other substance (relative retention time 0.56).

Hydriodic acid (49 percent) reacted immediately with a solution of MIB in acetone to give a product that showed a single crimson spot (R_f 0.96) on thin-layer chromatography. The product in chloroform showed infrared absorption at 3080 (medium), 1740 (weak), 1655 (medium), and 880 cm^{-1} (strong) corresponding to a methylene with standard absorption at 3080 (medium), 1800 ∿ 1750 (medium), 1655 (medium), and 890 cm^{-1} (strong) (Nakanishi, 1962). Again an olefin was produced rather than the desired ester.

61

In contrast, hydrobromic acid (22 percent) reacted almost completely with MIB in ethanol in 30 min at room temperature to produce little olefin. The major product had a gas chromatographic retention time relative to that of methylisoborneol of 1:10 and gave a crimson spot on thin-layer chromatography with a slightly smaller R_f (0.42) than that of MIB (0.49). The major change in the infrared absorption in potassium bromide was a shift of the C-O stretching band from 1095 cm^{-1} in MIB to 1030 cm^{-1} in the product, and this indicated transformation of the tertiary alcohol to a secondary (Nakanishi, 1962). Both the chromatographic and the infrared evidence indicate rearrangement of the MIB to a secondary alcohol, possible 4-methylisoborneol (Toivonen, 1968).

These failures to develop a suitable derivative to use with the electron-capture detector meant that we were forced to use the flame ionization detector. To get the desired sensitivity for trace concentrations of MIB in water, the techniques explained below had to be developed to make extreme concentrations of water extracts.

Extraction

MIB resembles its precursor camphor in volatility, in gas chromatographic retention times, and in having extremely high distribution ratios for partitioning into organic solvents from water. Camphor then quickly became our choice as internal standard in the analysis of MIB.

The favorable partitioning into organic solvents meant that usually only small proportions of extractant (1-2 percent) were necessary to extract MIB from water, and this helped both to reduce the amount of coextractives and also the degree of concentration necessary before analysis. However, considerable concentration was still necessary and this severely limited the choice of solvent for extraction. MIB co-distills with some solvents and with others the grade readily available has impurities that concentrate sufficiently to cause interference with the analysis. Chloroform was quite satisfactory for analysis down to about 1 μg/l but below this solvent impurities tended to interfere. Methylene chloride was entirely satisfactory and in addition was readily removed because of its outstanding volatility.

Concentration of Extracts

To achieve the desired sensitivity of 0.1 μg/l for MIB in water, it was evident that the extract from 1 liter of water would have to be concentrated to as little as 20 μl before gas chromatography. Because both MIB and camphor readily sublime, special attention had to be given to the method of concentration.

Removal of solvent through a micro Snyder distillation column (Figure 5) was first tried. This method has the advantage that several samples can be concentrated simultaneously with little attention and at the end of evaporation the appartus is self-rinsing (Burke et al., 1966). Concentration vessels of the type A and B shown in Figure 5 were used. These were fabricated from 25 ml round-bottomed flasks and comfortably held the 20 ml of solvent from the extraction of 1 liter of water for MIB. With type A, access to the concentrate with a syringe was a little awkward but it was generally preferred because of its simplicity. Type B had to be assembled with water as a seal on the lower joint to avoid small losses during the concentration, but was advantageous in that the lower tube could be removed later for easy access to the concentrate. The smallest volume attainable with this apparatus was about 200 µl, which was sufficiently low to allow analyses down to about 1 µg/l.

Both relative and absolute recoveries for the evaporation were determined using 1-10 µg of MIB in 20 ml of various solvents. Absolute recoveries were determined as near as possible from the volume of concentrate as calculated from its weight. Disappointingly, pentane and hexane gave only about 50 percent absolute recoveries and relative recoveries were very erratic. However, methylene chloride, chloroform, and carbon tetrachloride gave quantitative absolute and relative recoveries. Of these latter solvents, methylene chloride was the obvious choice for the analysis because of its greater volatility and availability in pure grades.

To attain the highest sensitivity desired, it was necessary to determine how to reduce the initial concentrate of 200 µl to about 20 µl without loss of MIB. This was attempted initially in the lower tube of vessel B by equipping this tube with a small Snyder column. Although relative recoveries were excellent absolute losses occurred which largely nullified the effect of solvent removal.

However, concentration of the initial concentrate in vessel A or the lower tube of B on a rotary evaporator without a heating bath was successful without loss of MIB or camphor. The same result was possible by simply connecting the vessels to a water aspirator, but then there was risk of losing the sample by bumping.

Evaporation of Column Eluates

Before carrying out the purification of the few milligrams of natural MIB available by liquid chromatography, losses were anticipated during the evaporation of the column eluate to dryness. However, preliminary tests with synthetic MIB showed that, although 2.5 mg in 50 ml of hexane was evaporated to dryness on a rotary evaporator at 45° with a recovery of only 30 percent, similar evaporation at 35° using methylene chloride gave nearly quantitative recovery. Accordingly, the liquid chromatography was worked out on the basis of methylene chloride as eluant.

Gas Chromatography

The initial parts of this work were carried out by gas chromatography using a commercially prepared glass column of 3 percent OV-1. First tests on the use of camphor as internal standard gave satisfactory results in the determination of MIB in water at 100 µg/l. However at 10 µg/l unfavorable adsorption effects were observed with the smaller amount of internal standard used. Peak height response relative to that of MIB decreased markedly and peak width and retention time increased to the point that resolution from MIB was mostly destroyed.

The column was therefore replaced with one of DMCS-treated glass packed with 3 percent SP-2100, a similar stationary phase to that of 3 percent OV-1 but with improved characteristics. No untoward adsorption effects were noted with the column. Providing it was not subjected to harsh heat treatment, this type of column proved to be very stable in performance over a period of many months.

In the quantitation of MIB in this work, peak height relative to camphor for the sample was compared with that of a standard mixture showing a similar ratio. Standard mixtures in ethanol were prepared by mixing a stock solution of MIB (10 mg/100 ml) with that of camphor (8 mg/100 ml) in various proportions. When stored in stoppered volumetric flasks at room temperature, they proved to be very stable over a period of many months. It was assumed that there was a linear relationship between the amount of MIB in the sample and the peak height ratio, and that this ratio was unaffected by dilution of the solution.

To substantiate these assumptions the response factor was determined for MIB from some standard reference mixtures and their corresponding 1:10 dilutions as shown in Table 9. Evidently the response factor is not appreciably affected by dilution. Also, although there is a slight fall in the response factor with the undiluted mixtures as the proportion of MIB is reduced greatly, this is not significant enough to affect accuracy if widely differing peak height ratios are not compared.

TABLE 9. RESPONSE FACTOR OF MIB FOR VARIOUS PROPORTIONS WITH THE INTERNAL STANDARD AND AMOUNTS GAS CHROMATOGRAPHED

Ratio of (A/A') volumes MIB stock solution to that of internal standard in reference mixture[1]	Amount of chromatographed, pg[2]		Peak height of MIB (H) relative to that of internal standard (Hi)	Response Factor $\frac{H}{Hi} \times \frac{Wi}{W}$
	MIB (W)	Internal Standard (Wi)		
2	133.3	53.33	2.15	0.860
	13.33	5.333	2.14	0.856
1	100.0	80.0	1.04	0.832
	10.00	8.000	1.05	0.840
0.2	33.33	133.3	0.196	0.784
	3.333	13.33	0.211	0.844

[1] Stock solution of MIB (A) = 10.0 mg/100 ml in ethanol.
[2] Internal standard solution (A') = 8.0 mg/100 ml
Two microliters of each reference mixture was chromatographed both undiluted and as a 1:10 dilution with ethanol.

Recoveries from Various Water Types

Recoveries of MIB added to various waters in a small amount of ethanol are given in Table 10. Blanks equivalent to 0.1 µg/l were carried out for these waters and also for a sample of lake water, but no interference was noted. A typical chromatogram from a recovery at 0.1 µg/l is shown in Figure 26.

TABLE 10. RELATIVE RECOVERY OF MIB FROM VARIOUS WATERS

Added, µg/l		Recovery of MIB, %, Relative to Camphor			
MIB	Camphor (internal standard)	Type of Water Used			
		Distilled	Tap	Well	Polluted Stream
10	4	100.0	97.8	98.2; 97.5	99.0
5	4		97.7; 94.9	97.4; 97.3	103.7
1	4	100.4	100.6	100.7	
1	0.4		96.6		
0.5	0.4		100.1		
0.1	0.8		101.8		
Mean relative recovery, % ± standard deviation		100.3±0.2	98.5±2.4	98.2±1.4	101.4±3.3

ADSORPTION OF MIB AND GEOSMIN[1]

Results

Isotherm data for MIB are shown in Figure 27. Included are the isotherms for MIB on F-200 carbon in the presence of both 10 and 100 mg/l of commercial humic acid. Because of the small dosages of carbon used in the tests, negligible reductions in humic acid concentration were observed and final concentrations were approximately the same as the initial

---

1. Much of the material in this subsection has been taken from "Activated Carbon Adsorption of the Odorous Compounds 2-Methylisoborneol and Geosmin" by D. R. Herzing, V. L. Snoeyink and N. F. Wood, Jour. Amer. Water Works Assoc., 69, 223 (1977), with the permission of the copyright owner.

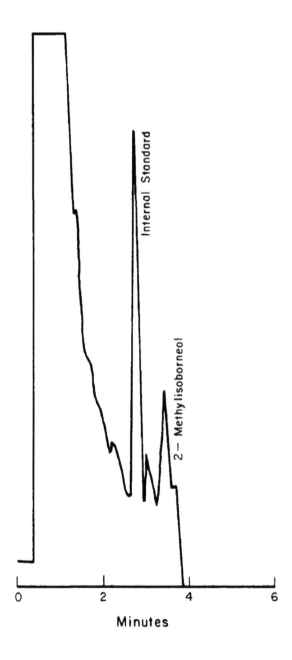

Figure 26. Chromatogram obtained in a study of the recovery of MIB added to tap water at 0.1 µg/l.

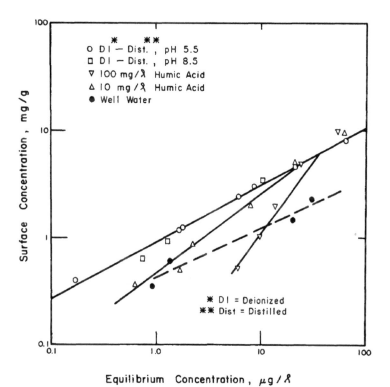

Figure 27. Adsorption of MIB.

concentrations. One hundred mg/l is unrealistic for most natural waters (typical values are on the order of 1 to 10 mg/l) but the data are useful for emphasizing the magnitude of the competitive effect. As the equilibrium concentration of MIB increases, the isotherms for MIB in the presence of humic acid converge to the isotherm for which there is no competition. However, the isotherm for MIB in well water does not converge in the concentration range studied, probably owing to the nature of the organic matter in the well water vs. the commercial humic acid used.

Batch adsorption tests using F-200 carbon were conducted with geosmin in a manner similar to that used for MIB and the results are shown in Figure 28. The data show that at an equilibrium geosmin concentration of 0.1 μg/l the capacity of the carbon is 0.54 mg/g in deionized-distilled water, twice the capacity shown in Figure 27 for MIB at the same equilibrium concentration. The data for adsorption of geosmin from 10 and 40 mg/l humic acid solution are also shown and indicate a greater degree of competition than there was with MIB. In fact, at 1 μg/l equilibrium concentration in the presence of 10 mg/l humic acid, the surface concentration of geosmin is essentially the same as for MIB under the same conditions.

Adsorption data were also obtained for MIB and geosmin in deionized-distilled water using a single test bottle and sequential addition of adsorbate, with equilibration after each addition, as described in Section 4. The data obtained in both cases varied only slightly from the data which are shown in Figures 28 and 29.

Figure 29 shows the results of several continuous flow column experiments in which MIB was the adsorbate and F-200 was the carbon. An obvious characteristic of these curves is the manner in which they level off rather than converge to $C/C_0 = 1$. This suggests that a portion of the capacity is being utilized very slowly and that a long operation time would be required for complete saturation. This effect is probably attributable to a combination of the high flow rate, short contact time and a slower rate of mass transport in the small pores of the carbon. As predicted from the isotherms, the presence of 10 mg/l of humic acid greatly reduces the capacity of the carbon for MIB. The data show very little effect due to variation in pH from 5.5 to 8.5, also consistent with the isotherms. The divergence of the curve for pH 5.5 with no humic acid from the other curves after 40 hours is attributed to a decreased flow rate because of column plugging. Copper ion which was introduced to eliminate possible biological activity in the column appears to have no significant effect on the breakthrough curve.

Figure 29 also shows data for a column test in which geosmin was the adsorbate. The greater capacity observed for geosmin compared to MIB is consistent with the batch equilibrium data shown in Figures 27 and 28 which show geosmin to be more strongly adsorbed.

The data used to determine the C/C_0 plot for geosmin in Figure 29 are shown in Figure 30. As is apparent, geosmin loss from the open reservoir was significant and amounted to more than 40 percent over the 190 hr of the test. By comparison, MIB is much less volatile from aqueous solution with typical losses amounting to less than 10 percent over 100 hours.

68

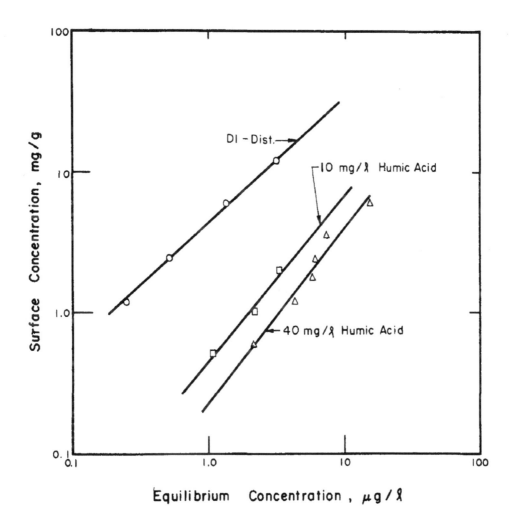

Figure 28. Adsorption of geosmin.

69

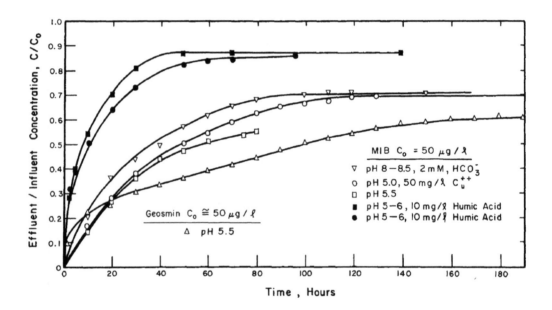

Figure 29. Column breakthrough curves for MIB and geosmin.

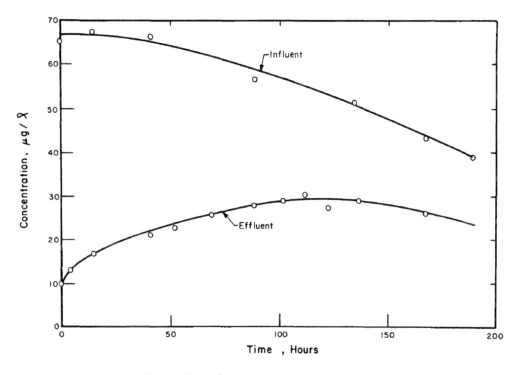

Figure 30.   Column breakthrough curve for geosmin.

Discussion

Even though earthy-musty odors are a common problem at water treatment plants and activated carbon is commonly used to remove these odors, it is difficult to say whether adsorption or biological activity, or some other mechanism, is effecting the removal. Our results show that two causative agents of earthy-musty odor, geosmin and MIB, are strongly adsorbed even in the presence of interfering natural organic matter.

Silvey et al. (1976) report that biological degradation of geosmin by *Bacillus cereus* readily takes place; because of the biological growth which develops in beds of GAC it is possible that some removal of earthy-musty odor can be attributed to it. Nevertheless, in our study biological activity did not contribute to geosmin or MIB removal. Most of the MIB (70-80 percent) and the geosmin (80-90 percent) was recovered unchanged through simple dioxane extraction of the carbon. No difference in percent recovery was noted when low pH systems were used with 50 mg/l of Cu^{2+} serving as a biocide as compared with systems near neutral pH without a biocide. Also, breakthrough curves were essentially the same when Cu^{2+} was used as when it was not.

It is not possible to conclude that the capacity of carbon in the column is the same as the carbon used in the batch tests because the columns were not run until saturation was achieved, although agreement at saturation is expected. When the column tests were terminated, approximately 50 percent of the expected saturation capacity for the column had been achieved. Lower flow rates would have resulted in less severe tailing for the breakthrough curve but longer experimental operation times would then be required to achieve a given degree of saturation and this would severely limit the number and variety of experiments which could be run.

The commercial humic acid used in this study significantly reduced the amount of the two odor compounds which would adsorb, with the effect being somewhat greater for the geosmin. Since humic acids are larger than fulvic acids and much larger than the odor compounds, it is possible that a greater reduction in adsorption capacity will take place in waters which have a larger amount of fulvic acids. The fulvic acids can penetrate smaller pores and thus may interfere with adsorption to a greater extent. However, as shown in the following subsections dealing with chlorophenols, the source of the fulvic acid is also likely to be important. Adsorption of MIB from well water showed a competitive effect somewhat different than that of commercial humic acid, and there was a strong indication that the organics in well water were more adsorbable.

An important question to be answered when GAC beds are used to remove trace organics concerns "unloading" of the carbon, or appearance of concentrations of substances in the effluents of GAC beds greater than are in the influent. This phenomenon is commonly observed for organic matter parameters such as COD and CCE while the GAC beds continue to remove odor (Love et al., 1973). To determine whether MIB would appear in the effluent if the humic acid concentration in the influent were suddenly increased, a column test was conducted, the results of which are shown in Figure 31. The bed

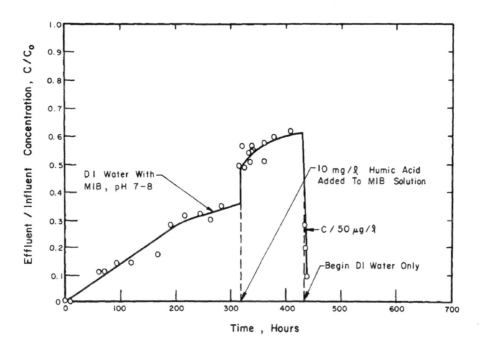

Figure 31. Column breakthrough curve for MIB.

contained 5 grams of F-200 carbon in a 1.27 cm diameter column. Bed depth was 7.6 cm and the flow rate was 2 liters/hr. As C/C_0 approached 0.4, 10 mg/l of humic acid was added to the influent MIB solution. The humic acid rapidly saturated the bed, with effluent concentration essentially equal to influent concentration after 70 hours. The effluent concentration of MIB increased more rapidly, as shown, but did not exceed the influent concentration. Unloading is expected only when no adsorption capacity remains to re-adsorb the MIB displaced by the humic acid.

After 430 hours all humic acid and MIB were eliminated from the influent solution and only deionized water was applied to the column. As shown in Figure 31, the effluent concentration dropped very rapidly. After passage of more than 200 bed volumes of water only a very small fraction of the total adsorbed MIB was released. The column run was terminated because of mechanical difficulties but the results indicate that MIB is not easily eluted from the carbon after adsorption.

A series of tests using MIB was conducted in a manner similar to the procedure normally used for determining isotherms except that they were not carried to equilibrium. All test solutions were agitated on a gyratory shaker for approximately 4 days. The results are presented in Figure 32, with the equilibrium curve for MIB adsorption from deionized-distilled water from Figure 27 reproduced for comparison. The data for these tests had much more scatter than did the equilibrium data and thus only the line of "best fit" is shown. A comparison of the curves for pH 5.5 in deionized-distilled water shows nearly 10 times as much MIB is adsorbed at equilibrium as at non-equilibrium. It is interesting to note that changing the pH from 5.5 to 8.5 again had little effect on the amount adsorbed, and that humic acid had a more significant effect than was observed at equilibrium conditions (see Figure 27). A major difference with the interference effect was that the curves with and without humic acid did not converge at high MIB concentrations as in the equilibrium case. Inclusion of 50 mg/l Cu^{2+} in the test solution as a biocide apparently increased the rate of adsorption, although there appears to be no good explanation for this phenomenon. As was previously noted, this effect was not observed in the column tests.

The importance of the non-equilibrium data is that when carbon is used under conditions where equilibrium is not achieved, such as is likely the case in many instances when PAC is used, the humic substances still have a major effect on adsorption capacity for MIB.

The results of our study show MIB and geosmin to be much more strongly adsorbed than natural organic matter. To illustrate this, if it is assumed that 10 μg/l of MIB and 10 mg/l of humic acid are present in water entering a 2 foot deep carbon bed at a flow rate of 2 gpm/ft², it would take on the order of 200 months to completely saturate the bed with MIB while saturation with the humic acid would take place in about 1 month. This calculation assumes that MIB and humic acid are present on a continuous basis and that all of the substance entering the bed is adsorbed until the bed is saturated. Of course, in an actual situation some leakage would take place before the bed was completely saturated; also, some trace compounds may be present

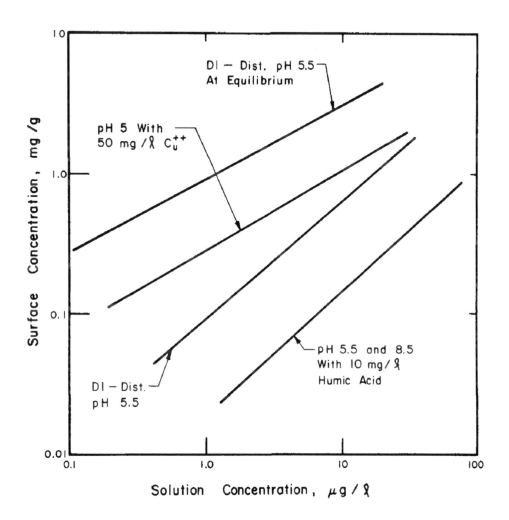

Figure 32.   Adsorption of MIB--nonequilibrium.

which also compete with MIB for adsorption sites. Factors which would tend
to make the bed life for MIB even longer are that earthy-musty odors generally occur periodically through the year and that biological growths may
develop in the bed which would destroy a fraction of the MIB. Larger scale
studies are needed to verify these predictions. All indications are that if
removal of MIB or geosmin is the sole objective for which GAC beds are used,
the bed life will be very long. Currently, data on MIB or geosmin distribution in full scale carbon beds are needed to verify that penetration of
these compounds through the bed is extremely slow.

ADSORPTION OF CHLOROPHENOL

As phenol becomes substituted with chlorine, its solubility decreases
and it is adsorbed more strongly onto carbon as was found by Gauntlett and
Packham (1973). Their results also indicated that the dissociated molecules
found at pH values above a weak acid's pK_a value are less strongly adsorbed
than the undissociated form. Ward and Getzen (1970) observed the same
effect of pH in a study performed on the adsorption of aromatic acids in
aqueous solution. They found that maximum adsorption occurred near the
point where pH = pK_a for each compound. Their data suggested that greater
quantities of undesirable solutes may be removed from waters by the addition
of carbon at a pH level slightly below this optimum point.

In the research reported herein, adsorption of chlorophenols is examined
down to the threshold odor level in systems containing single solute,
bisolute chlorophenol, and single solute chlorophenol in the presence of
various humic substances. Previous research has not examined these aspects
of chlorophenol adsorption.

Single Solute Systems

Equilibrium data for single solute isotherms of 2,4-DCP and 2,4,6-TCP
in distilled water at pH 5.2, 7.0 and 9.1 are shown in Figures 33 and 34.
At pH 5.2 and 7.0, 2,4-DCP is primarily undissociated (pK_a = 7.85) while
at pH 9.1 it is primarily anionic. At pH 5.2, 2,4,6-TCP is primarily
undissociated (pK_a = 6.0) while at pH 7.0 and 9.1 it is primarily anionic.
The effect of pH on adsorption capacity for an equilibrium concentration of
2×10^{-8} M chlorophenol species is shown on Figure 35. The results confirm
findings of Zogorski and Faust (1974) for 2,4-DCP in the millimolar concentration range. Adsorption of 2,4-DCP and 2,4,6-TCP rises to a maximum at
pH values near the compound's pK_a and falls off rapidly at pH values above
the pK_a. The peak in adsorption near pH = pK_a where the species is 50
percent ionized results because of synergistic adsorption of the anionic
and neutral species (Ward and Getzen, 1970). Jain and Snoeyink (1973) pro-
pose the alternative explanation that the anionic and neutral species adsorb
at two different kinds of sites thereby increasing the total amount of
adsorption when both species are present above that when one species pre-
dominates.

The results also confirm findings of Gauntlett and Packham (1973) in
that the more highly substituted the molecule is with chlorine, the better

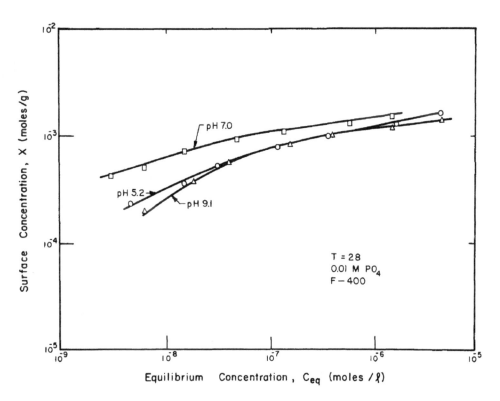

Figure 33. Adsorption isotherms for 2,4-dichlorophenol.

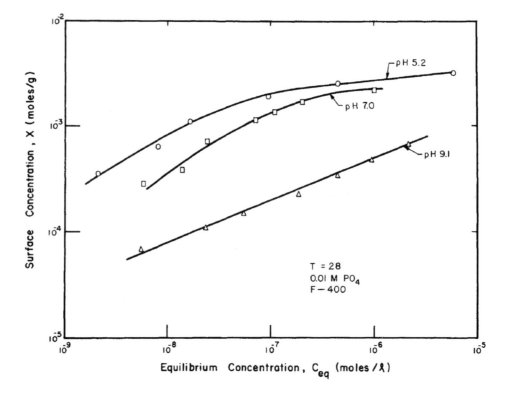

Figure 34. Adsorption isotherms for 2,4,6-trichlorophenol.

78

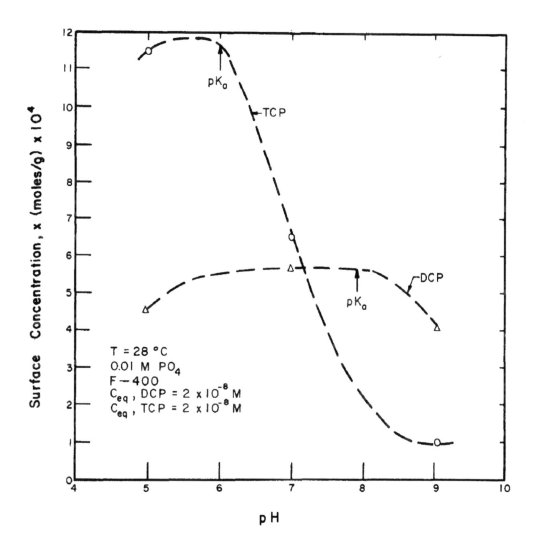

Figure 35. Influence of pH on chlorophenol adsorption capacity.

is the adsorption of the undissociated molecule. At pH 5.2, 2,4,6-TCP adsorbs three times as strongly as 2,4-DCP at an equilibrium concentration of 2×10^{-8} M. It should be noted that at each pH value studied, 10^{-2} M phosphate buffer was employed to ensure that the solution pH would remain constant throughout the time required to reach equilibrium. Zogorski and Faust (1976) reported that the adsorption of undissociated 2,4-DCP is unaffected by the presence of 5×10^{-2} M phosphates while the equilibrium capacities of dissociated 2,4-DCP were enhanced by about 10 to 20 percent. Due to the sensitivity of adsorption to pH fluctuations in the region near the pK_a of the chlorophenols, it was felt that use of the buffer was more important than its potential for causing a shifting adsorption capacity.

An attempt was made to fit the experimental single solute data with the Langmuir adsorption equation shown below. The model assumes that a mono-layer of solute molecules is adsorbed on the surface, the energy of adsorption is constant, and that no interaction occurs between adsorbed molecules (Langmuir, 1918).

$$X = \frac{X_m \, b \, C_{eq}}{1 + b \, C_{eq}} \tag{1}$$

where:

X = amount of solute adsorbed per unit weight of adsorbent

X_m = surface coverage corresponding to a monolayer of adsorbate molecules on the adsorbent surface

b = constant related to energy of adsorption, where $1/b$ is the adsorbate concentration at which adsorption attains one-half of the monolayer coverage

C_{eq} = equilibrium solute concentration

Linearization of Equation 1 results in the following form:

$$\frac{1}{X} = \frac{1}{X_m} + \frac{1}{b \, X_m \, C_{eq}} \tag{2}$$

Fit of the data to the Langmuir model is indicated if the plot of $1/X$ versus $1/C_{eq}$ is linear. It was found that the data presented in Figures 33 and 34 did not adhere to the model over the concentration range studied, as was observed in several other studies (Zogorski and Faust, 1974; Snoeyink et al., 1969). Instead, a computer program was used to fit the data to a polynomial by Gaussian elimination and least-squares analysis. The data fit a second order polynomial of the form:

$$\ln (X) = J + K \ln (C_{eq}) + L (\ln C_{eq})^2 \tag{3}$$

The constants obtained for each isotherm are listed in Table 11.

TABLE 11. VALUES OF CONSTANTS FOR EQUATION 3 FOR
CHLOROPHENOL SINGLE SOLUTE DATA

Compound	Solution pH	J	K	L
2,4-DCP	5.2	-8.4904	-0.48105	-0.02470
	7.0	-6.9126	-0.22529	-0.01375
	9.1	-14.056	-1.2068	-0.048154
2,4,6-TCP	5.2	-11.646	-0.96124	-0.038926
	7.0	-13.201	-1.1995	-0.049262
	9.1	-0.19919	+0.66134	+0.0086726

Bisolute Systems

Many studies of carbon adsorption from single solute systems have been conducted but natural waters contain a mixture of organic substances. As the study of the kinetics of phenol chlorination by Lee (1967) showed, there is commonly a number of chlorophenols present at a given time, for example. The presence of other compounds results in the occurrence of competition for adsorption sites which can markedly affect the adsorption of a particular substance. Mutual inhibition of adsorptive capacity occurs if the adsorption affinities of the solutes do not differ by more than a few orders of magnitude, and if there is no specific interaction between solutes which enhances adsorption (Weber and Morris, 1964). Some information can be obtained from simplified systems, such as bisolute systems, and other information can be obtained from studies using natural waters and simulated natural waters.

The most common model used to predict equilibrium concentrations in a multi-solute system is the Langmuir model for competitive adsorption, first developed by Butler and Ockrent (1930). The model permits calculation of the amount of species "1" adsorbed per unit weight of adsorbent at equilibrium concentration $C_{eq,1}$ in the presence of other species.

$$X_1 = \frac{X_{m,1}\, b_1\, C_{eq,1}}{1 + \sum_{i=1}^{n} (b_i\, C_{eq,i})} \qquad (4)$$

The constants X_m and b in Equation 4 are those obtained from single solute systems. The Langmuir competitive model is not expected to apply to systems where adsorption of either component of a bisolute system occurs on sites that are either inaccessible or unavailable to one of the species, e.g., where a portion of the adsorption occurs without competition. If the Langmuir model for competitive adsorption does predict adsorption capacities from a bisolute system when $X_{m,1} \neq X_{m,2}$, it is probably because the species compete for all available sites. The difference in X_m values in this instance would most likely be caused by a difference in surface area covered by one adsorbate as compared with the competing adsorbate (Jain and Snoeyink, 1973)

Jain and Snoeyink (1973) studied competitive adsorption of bisolute mixtures of organic anions and neutral species. Typical results showed that the presence of 5×10^{-3} M p-bromophenol reduced the capacity for p-nitrophenol by nearly 2 orders of magnitude at p-nitrophenol equilibrium concentration of 5×10^{-5} M. It was found that the Langmuir competitive model, which assumes competition among species for various sites could accurately describe the adsorption from a solution of these compounds in the neutral form. The data for other mixtures were varied, however. Some adsorbed with very little competition and in other cases, electrostatic repulsive forces were of importance. These latter cases are more difficult to describe with a model, although a modification of the Langmuir equation to account for some adsorption without competition was moderately successful. Their model is based on the assumption that adsorption occurs without competition when $X_{m,1} > X_{m,2}$ and that the number of sites for which there is no competition is equal to the quantity $(X_{m,1} - X_{m,2})$. The equation for the amount of species "1" adsorbed takes the form below while the equation for the amount of species "2" adsorbed is the same as that in the Langmuir model.

$$X_1 = \frac{(X_{m,1} - X_{m,2}) \, b_1 \, C_{eq,1}}{1 + b_1 \, C_{eq,1}} + \frac{X_{m,2} \, b_1 \, C_{eq,1}}{1 + b_1 \, C_{eq,1} + b_2 \, C_{eq,2}} \tag{5}$$

Tables 12, 13 and 14 show equilibrium data obtained for competitive adsorption studies using 2,4-DCP and 2,4,6-TCP at pH 5.2, 7.0, and 9.1. Three different isotherms were set up at each pH to attempt to show the magnitude of competition between each species by increasing the equilibrium concentration of one species relative to the other. To indicate the degree of competition, the amount which would be adsorbed per gram if the species were present in solution alone, X_{ss}, is tabulated. Also tabulated is the extent of adsorption as predicted by the Langmuir and the Jain and Snoeyink competitive models, Equations 4 and 5, respectively. A computer program was developed to evaluate the constants for the models using the polynomials which were fitted to the single solute data. The program calculates X_m and b for each individual concentration and then uses these values in Equations 4 and 5 to calculate the amount of species adsorbed in the presence of the other chlorophenol.

TABLE 12. CHLOROPHENOL COMPETITION AT pH 5.2

A. $C_{eq,DCP} \cong 0.35\ C_{eq,TCP}$

   $C_{o,DCP} = 2.70$ mg/l

   $C_{o,TCP} = 20.80$ mg/l

2,4-Dichlorophenol

Bottle	$C_{eq,DCP}$ mole/l	$C_{eq,TCP}$ mole/l	X_{obs} mole/g	X_{ss} mole/g	$X_{Langmuir}$ mole/g	X_{Jain} mole/g
1	5.52×10^{-9}	2.28×10^{-8}	1.62×10^{-4}	2.47×10^{-4}	1.51×10^{-4}	1.51×10^{-4}
2	2.01×10^{-8}	7.09×10^{-8}	2.13×10^{-4}	4.61×10^{-4}	2.38×10^{-4}	2.38×10^{-4}
3	3.99×10^{-8}	1.47×10^{-7}	2.71×10^{-4}	6.09×10^{-4}	2.82×10^{-4}	2.82×10^{-4}
4	1.61×10^{-7}	3.92×10^{-7}	3.31×10^{-4}	9.20×10^{-4}	3.94×10^{-4}	3.94×10^{-4}
5	6.44×10^{-7}	1.54×10^{-6}	3.77×10^{-4}	1.25×10^{-3}	3.60×10^{-4}	3.60×10^{-4}
6	3.37×10^{-6}	7.34×10^{-6}	3.77×10^{-4}	1.66×10^{-3}	3.99×10^{-4}	3.99×10^{-4}

2,4,6-Trichlorophenol

Bottle	$C_{eq,TCP}$ mole/l	$C_{eq,DCP}$ mole/l	X_{obs} mole/g	X_{ss} mole/g	$X_{Langmuir}$ mole/g	X_{Jain} mole/g
1	2.28×10^{-8}	5.52×10^{-9}	1.03×10^{-3}	1.22×10^{-3}	7.64×10^{-4}	1.04×10^{-3}
2	7.09×10^{-8}	2.01×10^{-8}	1.36×10^{-3}	1.87×10^{-3}	1.15×10^{-3}	1.55×10^{-3}
3	1.47×10^{-7}	3.99×10^{-8}	1.72×10^{-3}	2.20×10^{-3}	1.45×10^{-3}	1.91×10^{-3}
4	3.92×10^{-7}	1.61×10^{-7}	2.12×10^{-3}	2.50×10^{-3}	1.82×10^{-3}	2.32×10^{-3}
5	1.54×10^{-6}	6.44×10^{-7}	2.56×10^{-3}	2.91×10^{-3}	2.48×10^{-3}	2.84×10^{-3}
6	7.34×10^{-6}	3.37×10^{-6}	2.80×10^{-3}	3.42×10^{-3}	2.63×10^{-3}	2.89×10^{-3}

X_{obs} = observed X $X_{Langmuir}$ = X as calculated from Equation 4

X_{ss} = single solute X X_{Jain} = X as calculated from Equation 5

(continued)

TABLE 12 (continued)

B. $C_{eq,DCP} \cong 1.1\ C_{eq,TCP}$

$C_{o,DCP} = 3.68$ mg/l

$C_{o,TCP} = 8.11$ mg/l

2,4-Dichlorophenol

Bottle	$C_{eq,DCP}$ mole/l	$C_{eq,TCP}$ mole/l	X_{obs} mole/g	X_{ss} mole/g	$X_{Langmuir}$ mole/g	X_{Jain} mole/g
1	4.60×10^{-9}	8.78×10^{-9}	2.14×10^{-4}	2.28×10^{-4}	1.54×10^{-4}	1.54×10^{-4}
2	1.47×10^{-8}	1.57×10^{-8}	3.39×10^{-4}	3.95×10^{-4}	2.52×10^{-4}	2.52×10^{-4}
3	3.80×10^{-8}	3.14×10^{-8}	4.46×10^{-6}	6.00×10^{-4}	3.51×10^{-4}	3.51×10^{-4}
4	1.87×10^{-7}	1.16×10^{-7}	6.31×10^{-4}	9.61×10^{-4}	5.41×10^{-4}	5.41×10^{-4}

2,4,6-Trichlorophenol

Bottle	$C_{eq,TCP}$ mole/l	$C_{eq,DCP}$ mole/l	X_{obs} mole/g	X_{ss} mole/g	$X_{Langmuir}$ mole/g	X_{Jain} mole/g
1	8.78×10^{-9}	4.60×10^{-9}	3.89×10^{-4}	7.40×10^{-4}	4.77×10^{-4}	6.58×10^{-4}
2	1.57×10^{-8}	1.47×10^{-8}	6.17×10^{-4}	1.01×10^{-3}	5.94×10^{-4}	8.24×10^{-4}
3	3.14×10^{-8}	3.80×10^{-8}	8.13×10^{-4}	1.41×10^{-3}	7.69×10^{-4}	1.07×10^{-3}
4	1.16×10^{-7}	1.87×10^{-7}	1.16×10^{-3}	2.10×10^{-3}	1.16×10^{-3}	1.60×10^{-3}

Note: See Table 12A for definition of terms.

(continued)

TABLE 12 (continued)

C. $C_{eq,DCP} \cong 8.9 \, C_{eq,TCP}$

$C_{o,DCP} = 8.47$ mg/l

$C_{o,TCP} = 6.17$ mg/l

2,4-Dichlorophenol

Bottle	$C_{eq,DCP}$ mole/l	$C_{eq,TCP}$ mole/l	X_{obs} mole/g	X_{ss} mole/g	$X_{Langmuir}$ mole/g	X_{Jain} mole/g
1	2.61×10^{-8}	3.80×10^{-9}	4.98×10^{-4}	5.21×10^{-4}	3.68×10^{-4}	3.68×10^{-4}
2	9.20×10^{-8}	1.24×10^{-8}	6.82×10^{-4}	8.12×10^{-4}	5.45×10^{-4}	5.45×10^{-4}
3	1.75×10^{-7}	2.03×10^{-8}	8.55×10^{-4}	9.49×10^{-4}	6.54×10^{-4}	6.54×10^{-4}
4	4.75×10^{-7}	5.06×10^{-8}	1.00×10^{-3}	1.16×10^{-3}	8.23×10^{-4}	8.23×10^{-4}
5	1.47×10^{-6}	1.27×10^{-7}	1.24×10^{-3}	1.49×10^{-3}	1.02×10^{-3}	1.02×10^{-3}
6	5.24×10^{-6}	5.76×10^{-7}	1.50×10^{-3}	1.96×10^{-3}	1.12×10^{-3}	1.12×10^{-3}

2,4,6-Trichlorophenol

Bottle	$C_{eq,TCP}$ mole/l	$C_{eq,TCP}$ mole/l	X_{obs} mole/g	X_{ss} mole/g	$X_{Langmuir}$ mole/g	X_{Jain} mole/g
1	3.80×10^{-9}	2.61×10^{-8}	2.99×10^{-4}	4.65×10^{-4}	2.55×10^{-4}	3.14×10^{-4}
2	1.24×10^{-8}	9.20×10^{-8}	4.11×10^{-4}	8.90×10^{-4}	4.42×10^{-4}	5.73×10^{-4}
3	2.03×10^{-8}	1.75×10^{-7}	5.51×10^{-4}	1.14×10^{-3}	5.31×10^{-4}	6.98×10^{-4}
4	5.06×10^{-8}	4.75×10^{-7}	6.07×10^{-4}	1.66×10^{-3}	7.27×10^{-4}	9.91×10^{-4}
5	1.27×10^{-7}	1.47×10^{-6}	7.65×10^{-4}	2.15×10^{-3}	9.15×10^{-4}	1.29×10^{-3}
6	5.76×10^{-7}	5.34×10^{-6}	9.89×10^{-4}	2.61×10^{-3}	1.31×10^{-3}	1.87×10^{-3}

Note: See Table 12A for definition of terms.

(continued)

TABLE 12 (continued)

D. Data Summary

		Dichlorophenol				Trichlorophenol		
Bottle	C_{eq} mole/l	$\dfrac{X_{obs}}{X_{ss}}$	$\dfrac{X_{obs}}{X_{Langmuir}}$	$\dfrac{X_{obs}}{X_{Jain}}$	C_{eq} mole/l	$\dfrac{X_{obs}}{X_{ss}}$	$\dfrac{X_{obs}}{X_{Langmuir}}$	$\dfrac{X_{obs}}{X_{Jain}}$
Isotherm A: $C_{eq,DCP} \cong 0.35\, C_{eq,TCP}$								
1	5.52×10^{-9}	66%	107%	107%	2.28×10^{-8}	84%	135%	99%
2	2.01×10^{-8}	46	89	89	7.09×10^{-8}	73	118	88
3	3.99×10^{-8}	44	96	96	1.47×10^{-7}	78	119	90
4	1.61×10^{-7}	36	84	84	3.92×10^{-7}	85	116	91
5	6.44×10^{-7}	30	105	105	1.54×10^{-6}	88	103	90
6	3.37×10^{-6}	23	94	94	7.34×10^{-6}	82	106	97
Isotherm B: $C_{eq,DCP} \cong 1.1\, C_{eq,TCP}$								
1	4.60×10^{-9}	94	139	139	8.78×10^{-9}	53	82	59
2	1.47×10^{-8}	86	135	135	1.57×10^{-8}	61	104	75
3	3.80×10^{-8}	74	127	127	3.14×10^{-8}	58	106	79
4	1.87×10^{-7}	66	117	117	1.16×10^{-7}	55	100	73
Isotherm C: $C_{eq,DCP} \cong 8.9\, C_{eq,TCP}$								
1	2.61×10^{-8}	96	135	135	3.80×10^{-9}	64	117	95
2	9.20×10^{-8}	83	125	125	1.24×10^{-8}	46	93	72
3	1.75×10^{-7}	90	131	131	2.03×10^{-8}	45	97	74
4	4.75×10^{-7}	86	122	122	5.06×10^{-8}	37	83	61
5	1.47×10^{-6}	83	122	122	1.27×10^{-7}	36	84	59
6	5.34×10^{-6}	77	134	134	5.76×10^{-7}	38	75	53

Note: See Table 12A for definition of terms.

TABLE 13. CHLOROPHENOL COMPETITION AT pH 7.0

A. $C_{eq,DCP} \cong 0.14\ C_{eq,TCP}$

$C_{o,DCP} = 6.58$ mg/l

$C_{o,TCP} = 10.76$ mg/l

2,4-Dichlorophenol

Bottle	$C_{eq,DCP}$ mole/l	$C_{eq,TCP}$ mole/l	X_{obs} mole/g	X_{ss} mole/g	$X_{Langmuir}$ mole/g	X_{Jain} mole/g
1	5.37×10^{-9}	4.25×10^{-8}	4.61×10^{-4}	5.40×10^{-4}	3.99×10^{-4}	3.99×10^{-4}
2	1.17×10^{-8}	9.62×10^{-8}	5.81×10^{-4}	$6.90 \text{x}.0^{-4}$	4.64×10^{-4}	4.64×10^{-4}
3	2.58×10^{-8}	2.15×10^{-7}	7.19×10^{-4}	8.80×10^{-4}	5.22×10^{-4}	5.23×10^{-4}
4	6.87×10^{-8}	5.19×10^{-7}	8.50×10^{-4}	1.11×10^{-3}	5.77×10^{-4}	5.77×10^{-4}
5	2.58×10^{-7}	1.65×10^{-6}	1.02×10^{-3}	1.37×10^{-3}	5.39×10^{-4}	5.39×10^{-4}
6	1.27×10^{-6}	6.58×10^{-6}	1.18×10^{-3}	1.71×10^{-3}	2.54×10^{-4}	2.54×10^{-4}

2,4,6-Trichlorophenol

Bottle	$C_{eq,TCP}$ mole/l	$C_{eq,DCP}$ mole/l	X_{obs} mole/g	X_{ss} mole/g	$X_{Langmuir}$ mole/g	X_{Jain} mole/g
1	4.25×10^{-8}	5.37×10^{-9}	6.22×10^{-4}	9.60×10^{-4}	4.10×10^{-4}	6.71×10^{-4}
2	9.62×10^{-8}	1.17×10^{-8}	7.83×10^{-4}	1.25×10^{-3}	6.10×10^{-4}	9.74×10^{-4}
3	2.15×10^{-7}	2.58×10^{-8}	9.67×10^{-4}	1.37×10^{-3}	8.57×10^{-4}	1.31×10^{-3}
4	5.19×10^{-7}	6.87×10^{-8}	1.14×10^{-3}	2.15×10^{-3}	1.18×10^{-3}	1.67×10^{-3}
5	1.65×10^{-6}	2.58×10^{-7}	1.34×10^{-3}	1.39×10^{-3}	1.73×10^{-3}	2.09×10^{-3}
6	6.58×10^{-6}	1.27×10^{-6}	1.45×10^{-3}	1.70×10^{-3}	2.39×10^{-3}	2.49×10^{-3}

Note: See Table 12A for definition of terms.

(continued)

TABLE 13 (continued)

B. $C_{eq,DCP} \cong 0.45 \; C_{eq,TCP}$

$\quad$ $C_{o,DCP} = 8.16$ mg/l

$\quad$ $C_{o,TCP} = 6.14$ mg/l

2,4-Dichlorophenol

Bottle	$C_{eq,DCP}$ mole/l	$C_{eq,TCP}$ mole/l	X_{obs} mole/g	X_{ss} mole/g	$X_{Langmuir}$ mole/g	X_{Jain} mole/g
1	7.05×10^{-9}	1.06×10^{-8}	4.75×10^{-4}	5.84×10^{-4}	4.84×10^{-4}	4.84×10^{-4}
2	1.23×10^{-8}	4.35×10^{-8}	7.15×10^{-4}	7.00×10^{-4}	5.12×10^{-4}	5.12×10^{-4}
3	7.36×10^{-8}	1.49×10^{-7}	9.94×10^{-4}	1.12×10^{-3}	7.33×10^{-4}	7.33×10^{-4}
4	3.25×10^{-7}	5.98×10^{-7}	1.21×10^{-3}	1.41×10^{-3}	8.33×10^{-4}	8.33×10^{-4}
5	1.44×10^{-6}	2.53×10^{-6}	1.46×10^{-3}	1.75×10^{-3}	6.19×10^{-4}	6.19×10^{-4}

2,4,6-Trichlorophenol

Bottle	$C_{eq,TCP}$ mole/l	$C_{eq,DCP}$ mole/l	X_{obs} mole/g	X_{ss} mole/g	$X_{Langmuir}$ mole/g	X_{Jain} mole/g
1	1.06×10^{-8}	7.05×10^{-9}	2.95×10^{-4}	3.65×10^{-4}	1.64×10^{-4}	2.27×10^{-4}
2	4.35×10^{-8}	1.23×10^{-8}	4.44×10^{-4}	8.70×10^{-4}	3.91×10^{-4}	6.20×10^{-4}
3	1.49×10^{-7}	7.36×10^{-8}	6.15×10^{-4}	1.50×10^{-3}	6.61×10^{-4}	1.00×10^{-3}
4	5.98×10^{-7}	3.25×10^{-7}	7.40×10^{-4}	2.20×10^{-3}	1.11×10^{-3}	1.52×10^{-3}
5	2.53×10^{-6}	1.44×10^{-6}	8.55×10^{-4}	3.09×10^{-3}	1.87×10^{-3}	2.10×10^{-3}

Note: See Table 12A for definition of terms.

(continued)

Table 13 (continued)

C. $C_{eq,DCP} \cong 1.4\ C_{eq,TCP}$

   $C_{o,DCP} = 12.58$ mg/1

   $C_{o,TCP} = 4.98$ mg/1

2,4-Dichlorophenol

Bottle	$C_{eq,DCP}$ mole/1	$C_{eq,TCP}$ mole/1	X_{obs} mole/g	X_{ss} mole/g	$X_{Langmuir}$ mole/g	X_{Jain} mole/g
1	2.70×10^{-8}	2.03×10^{-8}	8.45×10^{-4}	8.90×10^{-4}	6.78×10^{-4}	6.78×10^{-4}
2	7.67×10^{-8}	6.08×10^{-8}	1.05×10^{-3}	1.15×10^{-3}	8.14×10^{-4}	8.14×10^{-4}
3	1.53×10^{-7}	1.42×10^{-7}	1.28×10^{-3}	1.28×10^{-3}	8.83×10^{-4}	8.83×10^{-4}
4	6.29×10^{-7}	3.92×10^{-7}	1.49×10^{-3}	1.54×10^{-3}	1.06×10^{-3}	1.06×10^{-3}
5	2.21×10^{-6}	1.37×10^{-6}	1.74×10^{-3}	1.74×10^{-3}	1.01×10^{-3}	1.01×10^{-3}
6	5.40×10^{-6}	3.14×10^{-6}	1.92×10^{-3}	2.20×10^{-3}	6.87×10^{-4}	6.87×10^{-4}

2,4,6-Trichlorophenol

Bottle	$C_{eq,TCP}$ mole/1	$C_{eq,DCP}$ mole/1	X_{obs} mole/g	X_{ss} mole/g	$X_{Langmuir}$ mole/g	X_{Jain} mole/g
1	2.03×10^{-8}	2.70×10^{-8}	2.76×10^{-4}	5.70×10^{-4}	2.28×10^{-4}	2.97×10^{-4}
2	6.08×10^{-8}	7.67×10^{-8}	3.43×10^{-4}	1.03×10^{-3}	4.05×10^{-4}	5.80×10^{-4}
3	1.42×10^{-7}	1.53×10^{-7}	4.16×10^{-4}	1.50×10^{-3}	6.02×10^{-4}	8.81×10^{-4}
4	3.92×10^{-7}	6.29×10^{-7}	4.82×10^{-4}	2.02×10^{-3}	8.55×10^{-4}	1.19×10^{-3}
5	1.37×10^{-6}	2.21×10^{-6}	5.55×10^{-4}	2.39×10^{-3}	1.33×10^{-3}	1.64×10^{-3}
6	3.14×10^{-6}	5.40×10^{-6}	5.90×10^{-4}	2.52×10^{-3}	1.91×10^{-3}	2.06×10^{-3}

Note: See Table 12A for definition of terms.

(continued)

TABLE 13 (continued)

D. Data Summary

		Dichlorophenol				Trichlorophenol		
Bottle	C_{eq} mole/l	$\dfrac{X_{obs}}{X_{ss}}$	$\dfrac{X_{obs}}{X_{Langmuir}}$	$\dfrac{X_{obs}}{X_{Jain}}$	C_{eq} mole/l	$\dfrac{X_{obs}}{X_{ss}}$	$\dfrac{X_{obs}}{X_{Langmuir}}$	$\dfrac{X_{obs}}{X_{Jain}}$

Isotherm A: $C_{eq,DCP} \cong 0.14\ C_{eq,TCP}$

1	5.37×10^{-9}	85%	116%	116%	4.25×10^{-8}	65%	152%	93%
2	1.17×10^{-8}	84	125	125	9.62×10^{-8}	63	128	80
3	2.58×10^{-8}	82	137	137	2.15×10^{-7}	71	113	74
4	6.87×10^{-8}	77	147	147	5.19×10^{-7}	53	97	68
5	2.58×10^{-7}	74	189	189	1.65×10^{-6}	96	78	64
6	1.27×10^{-6}	69	465	465	6.58×10^{-6}	85	61	58

Isotherm B: $C_{eq,DCP} \cong 0.45\ C_{eq,TCP}$

1	7.05×10^{-9}	81	98	98	1.06×10^{-8}	81	180	130
2	1.23×10^{-8}	102	140	140	4.35×10^{-8}	51	114	72
3	7.36×10^{-8}	89	136	136	1.49×10^{-7}	41	93	62
4	3.25×10^{-7}	86	145	145	5.98×10^{-7}	34	67	49
5	1.44×10^{-6}	83	236	236	2.53×10^{-6}	28	46	41

Isotherm C: $C_{eq,DCP} \cong 1.4\ C_{eq,TCP}$

1	2.70×10^{-8}	95	125	125	2.03×10^{-8}	48	121	93
2	7.67×10^{-8}	91	129	129	6.08×10^{-8}	33	85	59
3	1.53×10^{-7}	100	145	145	1.42×10^{-7}	28	69	47
4	6.29×10^{-7}	97	141	141	3.92×10^{-7}	24	56	41
5	2.21×10^{-6}	100	172	172	1.37×10^{-6}	23	42	34
6	5.40×10^{-6}	87	279	279	3.14×10^{-6}	23	31	29

Note: See Table 12A for definition of terms.

TABLE 14. CHLOROPHENOL COMPETITION AT pH 9.1

A. $C_{eq,DCP} \cong 0.044\ C_{eq,TCP}$

   $C_{o,DCP} = 3.23$ mg/l

   $C_{o,TCP} = 4.64$ mg/l

2,4-Dichlorophenol

Bottle	$C_{eq,DCP}$ mole/l	$C_{eq,TCP}$ mole/l	X_{obs} mole/g	X_{ss} mole/g	$X_{Langmuir}$ mole/g	X_{Jain} mole/g
1	1.38×10^{-8}	1.62×10^{-7}	1.90×10^{-4}	3.35×10^{-4}	1.85×10^{-4}	2.63×10^{-4}
2	1.84×10^{-8}	3.73×10^{-7}	2.57×10^{-4}	3.95×10^{-4}	2.26×10^{-4}	2.86×10^{-4}
3	2.94×10^{-8}	6.84×10^{-7}	3.30×10^{-4}	5.10×10^{-4}	3.00×10^{-4}	3.53×10^{-4}
4	3.68×10^{-8}	1.52×10^{-6}	4.12×10^{-4}	5.70×10^{-4}	3.46×10^{-4}	3.49×10^{-4}
5	7.51×10^{-8}	3.85×10^{-6}	5.45×10^{-4}	7.53×10^{-4}	5.01×10^{-4}	5.01×10^{-4}

2,4,6-Trichlorophenol

Bottle	$C_{eq,TCP}$ mole/l	$C_{eq,DCP}$ mole/l	X_{obs} mole/g	X_{ss} mole/g	$X_{Langmuir}$ mole/g	X_{Jain} mole/g
1	1.62×10^{-7}	1.38×10^{-8}	2.24×10^{-4}	2.37×10^{-4}	1.65×10^{-4}	1.65×10^{-4}
2	3.73×10^{-7}	1.84×10^{-8}	3.00×10^{-4}	3.30×10^{-4}	2.21×10^{-4}	2.21×10^{-4}
3	6.84×10^{-7}	2.94×10^{-8}	3.80×10^{-4}	4.25×10^{-4}	2.66×10^{-4}	2.66×10^{-4}
4	1.52×10^{-6}	3.68×10^{-8}	4.58×10^{-4}	5.80×10^{-4}	3.57×10^{-4}	3.57×10^{-4}
5	3.85×10^{-6}	7.51×10^{-8}	5.43×10^{-4}	8.70×10^{-4}	4.74×10^{-4}	5.50×10^{-4}

Note: See Table 12A for definition of terms.

(continued)

TABLE 14 (continued)

B. $C_{eq,DCP} \cong 0.21 \ C_{eq,TCP}$

$C_{o,DCP} = 7.67 \ mg/l$

$C_{o,TCP} = 2.89 \ mg/l$

2,4-Dichlorophenol

Bottle	$C_{eq,DCP}$ mole/l	$C_{eq,TCP}$ mole/l	X_{obs} mole/g	X_{ss} mole/g	$X_{Langmuir}$ mole/g	X_{Jain} mole/g
1	2.61×10^{-8}	7.50×10^{-8}	3.60×10^{-4}	4.75×10^{-4}	2.62×10^{-4}	4.08×10^{-4}
2	5.67×10^{-8}	2.58×10^{-7}	5.35×10^{-4}	6.90×10^{-4}	4.10×10^{-4}	5.58×10^{-4}
3	1.29×10^{-7}	1.00×10^{-6}	7.81×10^{-4}	8.80×10^{-4}	6.15×10^{-4}	7.19×10^{-4}
4	3.60×10^{-7}	2.63×10^{-6}	9.79×10^{-4}	1.10×10^{-3}	9.11×10^{-4}	9.55×10^{-4}
5	1.23×10^{-6}	5.19×10^{-6}	1.24×10^{-3}	1.32×10^{-3}	1.27×10^{-3}	1.27×10^{-3}

2,4,6-Trichlorophenol

Bottle	$C_{eq,TCP}$ mole/l	$C_{eq,DCP}$ mole/l	X_{obs} mole/g	X_{ss} mole/g	$X_{Langmuir}$ mole/g	X_{Jain} mole/g
1	7.50×10^{-8}	2.61×10^{-8}	1.11×10^{-4}	1.75×10^{-4}	1.16×10^{-4}	1.16×10^{-4}
2	2.58×10^{-7}	5.67×10^{-8}	1.64×10^{-4}	2.87×10^{-4}	1.66×10^{-4}	1.66×10^{-4}
3	1.00×10^{-6}	1.29×10^{-7}	2.27×10^{-4}	4.90×10^{-4}	2.44×10^{-4}	2.44×10^{-4}
4	2.63×10^{-6}	3.60×10^{-7}	2.52×10^{-4}	7.30×10^{-4}	2.76×10^{-4}	2.76×10^{-4}
5	5.19×10^{-6}	1.23×10^{-6}	2.56×10^{-4}	9.60×10^{-4}	1.93×10^{-4}	2.49×10^{-4}

Note: See Table 12A for definition of terms.

(continued)

TABLE 14 (continued)

C. $C_{eq,DCP} \cong 0.45 \, C_{eq,TCP}$

$C_{o,DCP} = 10.68$ mg/1

$C_{o,TCP} = 1.56$ mg/1

2,4 Dichlorophenol

Bottle	$C_{eq,DCP}$ mole/1	$C_{eq,TCP}$ mole/1	X_{obs} mole/g	X_{ss} mole/g	$X_{Langmuir}$ mole/g	X_{Jain} mole/g
1	3.76×10^{-8}	8.36×10^{-8}	5.89×10^{-4}	5.90×10^{-4}	3.22×10^{-4}	4.89×10^{-4}
2	7.21×10^{-8}	1.61×10^{-7}	7.18×10^{-4}	7.50×10^{-4}	4.55×10^{-4}	6.39×10^{-4}
3	1.44×10^{-7}	3.70×10^{-7}	8.85×10^{-4}	9.00×10^{-4}	6.29×10^{-4}	8.05×10^{-4}
4	3.22×10^{-7}	8.55×10^{-7}	1.08×10^{-3}	1.08×10^{-3}	8.61×10^{-4}	1.00×10^{-3}
5	6.60×10^{-7}	1.60×10^{-6}	1.19×10^{-3}	1.22×10^{-3}	1.08×10^{-3}	1.17×10^{-3}
6	1.35×10^{-6}	2.23×10^{-6}	1.33×10^{-3}	1.33×10^{-3}	1.28×10^{-3}	1.33×10^{-3}

2,4,6-Trichlorophenol

Bottle	$C_{eq,TCP}$ mole/1	$C_{eq,DCP}$ mole/1	X_{obs} mole/g	X_{ss} mole/g	$X_{Langmuir}$ mole/g	X_{Jain} mole/g
1	8.36×10^{-8}	3.76×10^{-8}	7.04×10^{-5}	1.82×10^{-4}	1.15×10^{-4}	1.15×10^{-4}
2	1.61×10^{-7}	7.21×10^{-8}	8.49×10^{-5}	2.37×10^{-4}	1.34×10^{-4}	1.34×10^{-4}
3	3.70×10^{-7}	1.44×10^{-7}	1.02×10^{-4}	3.31×10^{-4}	1.61×10^{-4}	1.61×10^{-4}
4	8.55×10^{-7}	3.22×10^{-7}	1.17×10^{-4}	4.65×10^{-4}	1.82×10^{-4}	1.82×10^{-4}
5	1.60×10^{-6}	6.60×10^{-7}	1.16×10^{-4}	6.00×10^{-4}	1.76×10^{-4}	1.76×10^{-4}
6	2.23×10^{-6}	1.35×10^{-6}	1.18×10^{-4}	6.87×10^{-4}	1.26×10^{-4}	1.26×10^{-4}

Note: See Table 12A for definition of terms.

(continued)

TABLE 14   (continued)

D.   Data Summary

Bottle	C_{eq} mole/l	$\dfrac{X_{obs}}{X_{ss}}$	$\dfrac{X_{obs}}{X_{Langmuir}}$	$\dfrac{X_{obs}}{X_{Jain}}$	C_{eq} mole/l	$\dfrac{X_{obs}}{X_{ss}}$	$\dfrac{X_{obs}}{X_{Langmuir}}$	$\dfrac{X_{obs}}{X_{Jain}}$
		Dichlorophenol				Trichlorophenol		
Isotherm A:	$C_{eq,DCP} \cong 0.044\ C_{eq,TCP}$							
1	1.38×10^{-8}	57%	103%	72%	1.62×10^{-7}	95%	136%	136%
2	1.84×10^{-8}	65	114	90	3.73×10^{-7}	91	136	136
3	2.94×10^{-8}	65	110	93	6.84×10^{-7}	89	143	143
4	3.68×10^{-8}	72	119	118	1.52×10^{-6}	79	128	128
5	7.51×10^{-8}	72	109	109	3.85×10^{-6}	62	115	99
Isotherm B:	$C_{eq,DCP} \cong 0.21\ C_{eq,TCP}$							
1	2.61×10^{-8}	76	137	88	7.50×10^{-8}	63	96	96
2	5.67×10^{-8}	78	131	96	2.58×10^{-7}	57	99	99
3	1.29×10^{-7}	89	127	109	1.00×10^{-6}	46	93	93
4	3.60×10^{-7}	89	108	103	2.63×10^{-6}	35	91	91
5	1.23×10^{-6}	94	98	98	5.19×10^{-6}	27	132	103
Isotherm C:	$C_{eq,DCP} \cong 0.45\ C_{eq,TCP}$							
1	3.76×10^{-8}	100	183	120	8.36×10^{-8}	39	61	61
2	7.21×10^{-8}	96	158	112	1.61×10^{-7}	36	63	63
3	1.44×10^{-7}	98	141	110	3.70×10^{-7}	31	63	63
4	3.22×10^{-7}	100	125	108	8.55×10^{-7}	25	64	64
5	6.60×10^{-7}	98	110	102	1.60×10^{-6}	19	66	66
6	1.35×10^{-6}	100	104	100	2.23×10^{-6}	17	94	94

Note: See Table 12A for definition of terms.

Competition at pH 5.2 --

At pH 5.2 both 2,4-DCP and 2,4,6-TCP are primarily undissociated. Table 12 shows data obtained in competitive studies. As the equilibrium concentration of 2,4,6-TCP rises relative to the equilibrium concentration of 2,4-DCP the extent of adsorption of 2,4-DCP decreases relative to the single solute value, as summarized in Table 12D. The same phenomenon was observed for 2,4,6-TCP in relation to its single solute surface concentration values which indicates that competition for the same sites on the carbon is occurring. For both species, as the equilibrium concentrations increase with the ratio of their concentrations remaining constant, the extent of adsorption becomes increasingly lower than the single solute value suggesting that at the higher surface coverage the competition is more intense.

Table 12D shows the fit of the Langmuir and Jain and Snoeyink competitive models. The Langmuir model does a fairly good job of fitting both data sets. Since $X_{m,TCP}$ is greater than $X_{m,DCP}$ over the entire concentration range, the Jain model was applicable to the 2,4,6-TCP data. The Jain and Snoeyink model provided a better fit of the data where $C_{eq,TCP} > C_{eq,DCP}$ but did not improve the fit where $C_{eq,TCP} \simeq C_{eq,DCP}$. As the amount of 2,4,6-TCP increased the amount of anionic species increases since the pH is fairly close to the pK_a. The better fit of the Jain model where there is a significant portion of anionic TCP may indicate that there is some adsorption occurring without competition because of differences in adsorption sites for anionic versus neutral 2,4,6-TCP. Figures 36 and 37 show Langmuir model predictions for 2,4-DCP and 2,4,6-TCP as simulated using the computer and the single solute data previously presented in Figures 33 and 34.

Competition at pH 7.0 --

At pH 7.0, 2,4-DCP is primarily neutral while 2,4,6-TCP is primarily anionic. Table 13 shows data obtained in three studies at this pH value. As at pH 5.2, competition occurs between the species as evidenced by the increasing reduction of X_{obs} relative to X_{ss} as the equilibrium concentration of the competing species increases. As at pH 5.2, as the individual equilibrium concentrations increase with their ratio remaining approximately equal, the extent of adsorption is lowered significantly. The Langmuir model fits the 2,4-DCP data fairly well at low C_{eq} but at high C_{eq} values the fit is poor. The same is true for 2,4,6-TCP. At all of the concentrations studied, $X_{m,TCP}$ is greater than $X_{m,DCP}$ so the Jain and Snoeyink model applied. The Jain and Snoeyink model fit the data well for low 2,4,6-TCP concentrations but did not provide an improved fit at high concentrations. The Langmuir model predicted much less competition than was observed for 2,4-DCP; in some cases where $C_{eq,DCP} > 10^{-6}$ M the observed extent of adsorption was as much as 200 percent of that predicted by the model as shown in Table 13D. At high equilibrium concentrations of 2,4,6-TCP the observed extent of adsorption was less than predicted while at low equilibrium concentrations the opposite was true. For isotherm A where $C_{eq,DCP} \simeq 0.14$ $C_{eq,TCP}$, at low equilibrium concentrations, the Jain model did a good job of predicting extent of adsorption. Apparently the anionic 2,4,6-TCP and neutral 2,4-DCP which predominated here did not compete entirely for the

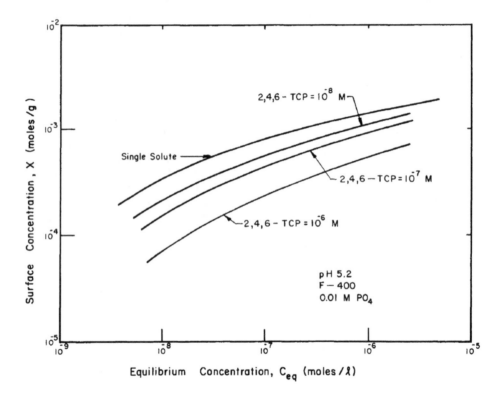

Figure 36. Competitive adsorption capacities predicted by the Langmuir model for dichlorophenol at pH 5.2.

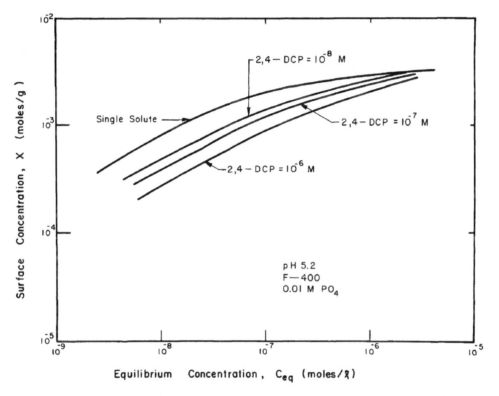

Figure 37. Competitive adsorption capacities predicted by the Langmuir
model for trichlorophenol at pH 5.2.

97

same sites. However at higher equilibrium concentrations the model failed since 2,4-DCP extent of adsorption was much greater than predicted while 2,4,6-TCP adsorbed lower than predicted. These same trends are evident in isotherms B and C which represent increasing concentrations of 2,4,6-TCP relative to 2,4-DCP. Since the pH is near the pK_a of both compounds the system contains four types of species, anionic 2,4-DCP and 2,4,6-TCP and neutral 2,4-DCP and 2,4,6-TCP which complicates the search for a reason for this behavior. In studies performed by Jain and Snoeyink (1973) on neutral p-nitrophenol and anionic benzenesulfonate, at pH 3.8, their model fit well for data collected in the concentration range 10^{-5} to 10^{-2} M which suggested that some adsorption occurred without competition. Neither species competed with the other to a great extent. However with neutral 2,4-DCP and anionic 2,4,6-TCP, 2,4-DCP competes with 2,4,6-TCP while 2,4,6-TCP affects 2,4-DCP only slightly. A possible explanation is that the anionic 2,4-DCP which is present at pH 7.0 effectively competes with the anionic 2,4,6-TCP while the anionic 2,4,6-TCP present does not compete with the neutral 2,4-DCP for the same sites. The small degree of competition of 2,4,6-TCP with 2,4-DCP occurs between the neutral species of which 2,4-DCP is present to a greater extent. The effective competition of anionic 2,4-DCP with 2,4,6-TCP occurs, as explained by Ward and Getzen (1969), since the anionic 2,4-DCP adsorption is favored at pH values just below a compound's pK_a. An alternative explanation may be that the chlorophenol species are changing on the carbon surface. Computer predictions for pH 7.0 are shown in Figures 38 and 39.

Competition at pH 9.1 --

At pH 9.1 both species are primarily anionic. Table 14 indicates that as the concentration of 2,4-DCP approaches that of 2,4,6-TCP the extent of adsorption of 2,4,6-TCP decreases. When $C_{eq,DCP} \cong 0.45\ C_{eq,TCP}$ the observed value of the extent of adsorption of 2,4-DCP is equal to the values which would be observed if 2,4,6-TCP were not present while those of 2,4,6-TCP are approximately 30 percent of those if no 2,4-DCP were present. Since the adsorption capacities for 2,4-DCP at this pH are nearly four times greater than those for 2,4,6-TCP, an explanation for which is not apparent, the X_m value also was greater indicating that some adsorption of 2,4-DCP could occur without competition. This was indicated by the fit of the Jain and Snoeyink model to the 2,4-DCP data for all three isotherms as illustrated in Table 14D. The model fit the 2,4,6-TCP fairly well except when $C_{eq,DCP}$ became close to that of $C_{eq,TCP}$. In this instance the adsorption of $C_{eq,TCP}$ was somewhat less than predicted indicating that the stronger adsorbing species predominated, and that electrostatic repulsion on the carbon surface may have come into play causing less 2,4,6-TCP to be adsorbed. When $C_{eq,TCP} \cong 23\ C_{eq,DCP}$ the predictions for 2,4,6-TCP were slightly lower than observed which may also indicate that less repulsion on the surface was occurring since less of the stronger adsorbing species was present. Figures 40 and 41 show adsorption capacities for pH 9.1 as predicted by the Jain and Snoeyink model which was the model which provided the best fit for the system. Apparently for this system the species adsorbed on the same sites but due to the widely differing capacities of the carbon for the two species, some adsorption occurred without competition.

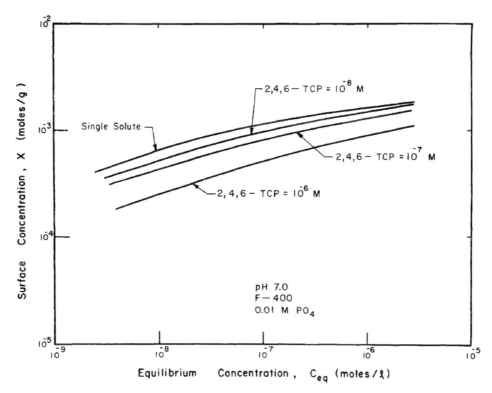

Figure 38. Competitive adsorption capacities predicted by the Langmuir model for dichlorophenol at pH 7.0.

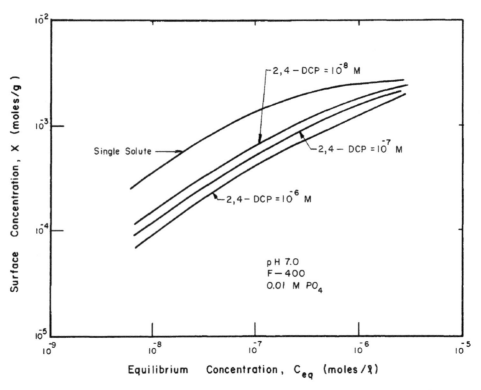

Figure 39. Competitive adsorption capacities predicted by the Langmuir model for trichlorophenol at pH 7.0.

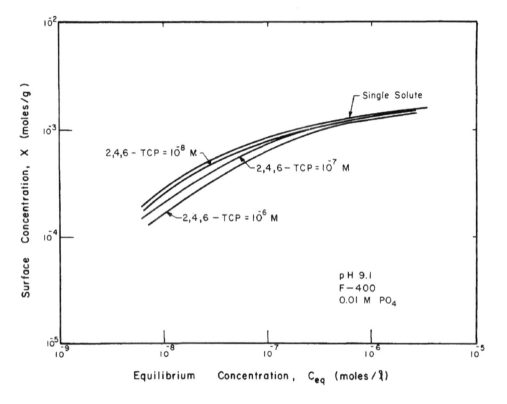

Figure 40. Competitive adsorption capacities predicted by the Jain model for dichlorophenol at pH 9.1.

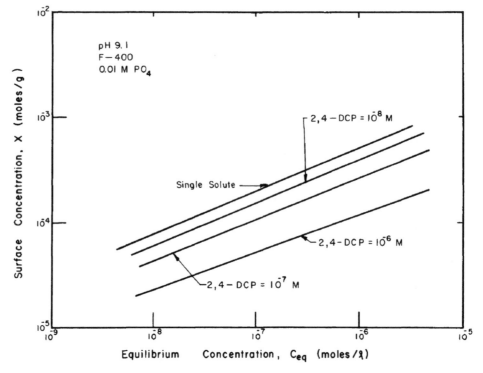

Figure 41. Competitive adsorption capacities predicted by the Jain model for trichlorophenol at pH 9.1.

According to Weber and Morris (1964), when the concentration of solute is small the term $(\sum_{i=1}^{n} b_i C_i)$ in the denominator of the Langmuir equation, Equation 4, is much less than unity so direct proportionality between solute equilibrium concentration and the amount adsorbed, X_i, is anticipated. No competitive effects would then be observed. However, this was not the case at pH 5.2 or at 7.0 or 9.1. In all instances for both compounds the term $(b_1 C_1 + b_2 C_2)$ was approximately equal to unity; as the value of C_i increased, the corresponding value of b_i decreased thus causing the entire denominator to remain greater than unity. In the Langmuir equation, the parameter b is proportional to $\exp(-\Delta H/RT)$ where ΔH is the adsorption energy. Adsorption energy varies with surface coverage; high-energy sites are occupied first with subsequent adsorption occurring at increasingly lower energy sites as the surface coverage increases. The net result is signifi-cant competition between adsorbates even at low concentration.

Chlorophenols in the Presence of Humic Substances

Data showing the adsorption of 2,4,6-TCP from solutions containing humic substances at pH 5.2 and 9.1 are shown in Tables 15 and 16, respec-tively. Three types of humic substances were used: commercial humic acid, leaf fulvic acid, and soil fulvic acid, the characteristics of which are described in Section 4 and previously in Section 5. Tests at each pH were performed with two initial concentrations of humic material, 10 and 50 mg/l as TOC, and also with two F-400 carbon doses to obtain different 2,4,6-TCP equilibrium concentrations. Since initial tests showed that 2,4-DCP behaved in a manner quite similar to 2,4,6-TCP in the presence of humic material, data were collected using 2,4,6-TCP as the sole chlorophenol adsorbate.

At pH 5.2, the presence of humic materials resulted in significant reductions in the capacity of carbon for 2,4,6-TCP as compared with that achieved in distilled water systems. Leaf fulvic acid proved to be the most effective competitor of the three humic substances tested while soil fulvic acid and commercial humic acids were nearly equally effective as competitors. As shown in Table 15, 10 mg/l of leaf fulvic acid reduced the carbon's capacity at $C_{eq} = 1.99 \times 10^{-6}$ M 2,4,6-TCP by 52 percent. Increasing the fulvic acid concentration to 50 mg/l resulted in a slightly greater reduction in 2,4,6-TCP capacity. Data for commercial humic and soil fulvic acids show the same trends. At a 2,4,6-TCP equilibrium con-centration of nearly an order of magnitude higher resulted in capacity reductions which were not quite as large.

It was expected that leaf fulvic acid and commercial humic acid would compete better with the chlorophenols than would soil fulvic acid due to their greater adsorbability as illustrated in Figure 16. The data in Figure 24 were collected at pH 7.0, however, so direct comparisons to the data collected at pH 5.2 cannot be drawn. Humic substance removal as measured by fluorescence showed the greatest removals for commercial humic acid and the least for soil fulvic acid. However, leaf fulvic acid was the best competitor with 2,4,6-TCP for adsorption sites while the other two materials resulted in roughly equivalent competition. Hence, percent

TABLE 15. 2,4,6-TCP COMPETITION WITH HUMIC SUBSTANCES - pH 5.2

C_{oTCP} = 23.80 mg/1

10^{-2} M phosphate buffer

Humic Substances			2,4,6-TCP			
Type	Initial Conc. mg/1 TOC	% Removed[1]	C_{eq} mole/1	X_{obs} mole/g	X_{ss} mole/g	X_{obs}/X_{ss}
Commercial Humic Acid	10	83	4.41×10^{-7}	1.50×10^{-3}	2.63×10^{-3}	57%
		70	5.01×10^{-6}	2.32×10^{-3}	3.40×10^{-3}	68
	50	66	1.08×10^{-6}	1.29×10^{-3}	2.68×10^{-3}	45
		48	9.18×10^{-6}	1.96×10^{-3}	3.55×10^{-3}	55
Leaf Fulvic Acid	10	56	1.99×10^{-6}	1.48×10^{-3}	3.11×10^{-3}	48
		37	1.04×10^{-5}	2.21×10^{-3}	3.60×10^{-3}	61
	50	28	3.80×10^{-6}	1.26×10^{-3}	3.31×10^{-3}	38
		16	1.73×10^{-5}	1.80×10^{-3}	3.72×10^{-3}	48
Soil Fulvic Acid	10	48	8.80×10^{-7}	1.50×10^{-3}	2.81×10^{-3}	53
		23	5.72×10^{-6}	2.30×10^{-3}	3.43×10^{-3}	67
	50	27	1.47×10^{-6}	1.27×10^{-3}	3.02×10^{-3}	42
		0	9.94×10^{-6}	1.94×10^{-3}	3.58×10^{-3}	54

[1]Percent removal as measured by fluorescence at pH 5.2.

Note: See Table 12A for definition of terms.

TABLE 16. 2,4,6-TCP COMPETITION WITH HUMIC SUBSTANCES - pH 9.1

$$C_{oTCP} = 23.80 \text{ mg/1}$$

10^{-2} M phosphate buffer

Humic Substances			2,4,6-TCP			
Type	Initial Conc. mg/1 TOC	% Removed[1]	C_{eq} mole/1	X_{obs} mole/g	X_{ss} mole/g	X_{obs}/X_{ss}
Commercial Humic Acid	10	75	1.05×10^{-7}	1.32×10^{-4}	2.06×10^{-4}	64
		59	1.32×10^{-6}	3.25×10^{-4}	5.30×10^{-4}	61
	50	57	2.35×10^{-7}	1.08×10^{-4}	1.80×10^{-4}	60
		39	2.55×10^{-6}	2.45×10^{-4}	6.90×10^{-4}	36
Leaf Fulvic Acid	10	61	1.01×10^{-7}	1.30×10^{-4}	2.04×10^{-4}	64
		42	1.53×10^{-6}	3.21×10^{-4}	5.55×10^{-4}	58
	50	44	1.72×10^{-7}	1.09×10^{-4}	2.47×10^{-4}	44
		22	2.25×10^{-6}	2.50×10^{-4}	6.40×10^{-4}	39
Soil Fulvic Acid	10	30	5.70×10^{-8}	1.30×10^{-4}	1.65×10^{-4}	79
		14	8.61×10^{-7}	2.35×10^{-4}	4.50×10^{-4}	74
	50	21	6.58×10^{-8}	1.10×10^{-4}	1.76×10^{-4}	62
		11	1.04×10^{-6}	2.69×10^{-4}	4.81×10^{-4}	56

[1]Percent removal as measured by fluorescence at pH 9.1.

Note: See Table 12A for definition of terms.

removal as determined by fluorescence apparently is not a good indicator of the ability of the humic substances tested to compete with chlorophenols. Further research is required to determine a parameter which better indicates the ability of the humic materials to compete with the chlorophenols.

Results for 2,4,6-TCP competition with humic substances at pH 9.1 are shown in Table 16. Commercial humic acid and leaf fulvic acid caused the greatest reduction in capacity for 2,4,6-TCP while soil fulvic acid was not as effective. Competition between the humic substances and 2,4,6-TCP was significant. For example, 10 mg/l leaf fulvic acid reduced the carbon's capacity at C_{eq} = 1.01 x 10^{-7} M by 36 percent while 50 mg/l leaf fulvic acid reduced the capacity at C_{eq} = 1.72 x 10^{-7} M by 56 percent. At a 2,4,6-TCP equilibrium concentration which is higher by an order of magnitude slightly greater reductions in capacity resulted which were unexpected. At pH 5.2, the opposite occurred, i.e., less competition was observed as the 2,4,6-TCP equilibrium capacity was increased. The reasons for this behavior are not clear at present. Percent removal of the humic substances as measured by fluorescence at pH 9.1 were lower than those at pH 5.2 which is consistent with the data shown in Figure 15 for the adsorption of soil fulvic acid as a function of pH.

The effect of pH on the ability of the humic materials to compete with 2,4,6-TCP is noteworthy. At pH 5.2 leaf fulvic acid was the strongest competitor while commercial humic and soil fulvic acids resulted in nearly equal competition. At pH 9.1, commercial humic and leaf fulvic acids competed more strongly with 2,4,6-TCP than did soil fulvic acid. Although more complete studies are needed, it is expected that the different molecular size distributions and functional group contents of the humic materials used in these studies lead to differences in adsorbabilities as a function of pH. This would explain the differences in competitive ability of the humic materials observed at pH 5.2 and 9.1.

Gauntlett and Packham (1973) investigated the adsorption of monochlorophenol at the 0.1 to 1 mg/l level in the presence of humic acid, fulvic acid and in Thames River water. They show a significant reduction in capacity (approximately 40 percent for the river water as compared with that achieved in distilled water systems) owing to the presence of these materials which is consistent with the results presented in this section. Unfortunately, they did not state the pH of their studies. In our study, for example, 10 mg/l soil fulvic acid at pH 5.2 reduced the capacity at C_{eq} = 8.80 x 10^{-7} M by 47 percent, while at pH 9.1 the capacity at C_{eq} = 8.61 x 10^{-7} M was reduced by only 26 percent. This can be accounted for by considering differences in adsorbabilities of soil fulvic acid at the two pH values; at pH 5.2, 48 percent of the soil fulvic acid was adsorbed while at pH 9.1 only 14 percent was removed. Therefore at pH 9.1 less material was competing with 2,4,6-TCP for adsorption sites than at pH 5.2

When the findings on competitive adsorption between chlorophenols and humic substances together with the information reported previously on competition between individual chlorophenols are considered, it is apparent that any testing to determine the best carbon and design criteria for a given application should be done using the natural water to be treated. Such factors as the nature and concentration of competing organic materials, pH and salt content of the water, among others, play a major role in determining the removal one can expect of a certain component.

ADSORPTION OF POLYNUCLEAR AROMATIC HYDROCARBONS

An initial test of the adsorbability of benzanthracene from water was made to first evaluate the effectiveness of the carbon. Solutions of various concentrations of benzanthracene were shaken with 10 mg of F-400 activated carbon for eight hours. After this time the concentrations were measured by fluorescence (see Table 17). Thus these extremely insoluble, non-polar compounds are adsorbed very well on active carbon.

TABLE 17. CONCENTRATIONS OF BENZANTHRACENE AFTER EIGHT HOURS

Volume (ml)	C_o ($\mu g/l$)	Concentration Remaining ($\mu g/l$)
150	242	12
150	50	<1
150	10	<1

Because the PAH was removed to below detection limits at such low dosages of carbon, the competitive effect of natural organic matter was examined. A kinetic study was performed to establish whether the presence of high concentrations of commercial humic acid would interfere with the rate of adsorption. Bottles with and without humic acid were set up with 1 mg/l of anthracene and taken off each day. A plot of the residual concentration vs. time both with and without humic acid is shown in Figure 28. No effect of the humic acid was observed. A series of bottles with 10 mg/l of carbon was set up with half of the bottles containing humic acid and anthracene and the other half with anthracene alone. Two bottles, one with and one without humic acid, were taken off the shaker each day and the anthracene concentrations were compared. Plots of residual concentration vs. time are shown in Figure 42. No effect of the humic acid was observed.

In our experiments we were using abnormally high concentrations of PAH. The anthracene was present as a particulate because concentrations exceeded the aqueous solubility of these extremely hydrophobic compounds. Even with large aqueous concentrations and extremely low carbon dosages we experienced removal of the PAH to below the detection limit, approximately 1 $\mu g/l$, after shaking for several days. It was believed that the PAH might associate with natural organic material in water and experience a decreased rate of adsorption or a decreased capacity on carbon. This was not found to be the case.

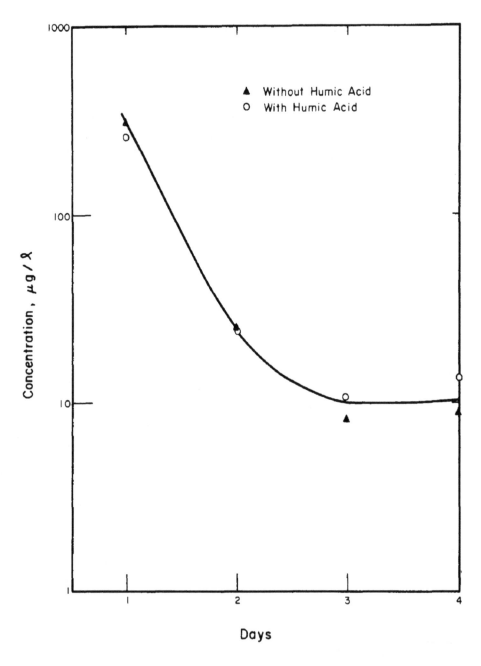

Figure 42. Kinetics of anthracene adsorption with and without humic acid

However, it should be stressed that our solutions were not natural and that the particles of anthracene in solution will not behave as individual molecules with respect to association with humic acid.

On this basis it does not appear likely that PAH will associate with relatively poorly adsorbable humic substances and result in the "leakage" of PAH from carbon beds. Based on a review of the literature as presented in Section 1, it is possible that other organics such as pesticides may penetrate carbon beds in this fashion.

REFERENCES

Andelman, J. B. 1973. World Health Organization, European Standard for Organic Matter in Drinking Water. In: Proc. 15th Water Quality Conference, *Organic Matter in Water Supplies: Occurrence, Significance and Control* (V. L. Snoeyink, ed.), University of Illinois, Urbana, IL. 70:55.

Burke, J. A., P. A. Mills, and D. C. Bostwick. 1966. *Jour. Assoc. Official Anal. Chem.* 49:999.

Burtschell, R. H., A. A. Rosen, F. M. Middleton, and M. B. Ettinger. 1959. Chlorine Derivatives of Phenol Causing Taste and Odor. *Jour. Amer. Water Works Assoc.* 51:205.

Butler, J. A. V. and C. Ockrent. 1930. Studies in Electrocapillarity. III. *Jour. Phys. Chem.* 34:2841.

Capmau, M. L., W. Chodkiewicz, and P. Cadiot. 1968. Stereochimie de l'Addition d'Organometalliques α et β Insatures sur le (t) Camphre. *Bull. Soc. Chim. France.* p. 3233.

Calgon Corp. 1969. Calgon Activated Carbon Product. Bull. No. 20-2a, Calgon Corp., Pittsburgh, PA.

Crosby, D. G. and A. S. Wong. 1973a. Photodecomposition of p-Chlorophenoxyacetic Acid. *Jour. Agr. Food Chem.* 21:1049.

Crosby, D. G. and A. S. Wong. 1973b. Photodecomposition of 2,4,5-Trichlorophenoxyacetic Acid (2,4,5-T) in Water. *Jour. Agr. Food Chem.* 21:1052.

Dice, J. C. 1976. The Challenge to the AWWA Taste and Odor Control Committee. Proc. AWWA Conference on Water Quality, Atlanta, Dec. 1975, AWWA, Denver, CO.

Dostal, K. A., R. C. Pierson, D. G. Hager and G. G. Robeck. 1965. Carbon Bed Design Criteria Study at Nitro, West Virginia. *Jour. Amer. Water Works Assoc.* 57:663.

Fieser, L. F. and G. Ourisson. 1953. Chromates d'alcools Tertiaires. *Bull. Soc. Chim. France.* p. 1152.

Friestad, H. O., D. E. Ott and F. A. Gunther. 1969. Automated Colorimetric Microdetermination of Phenols by Oxidative Coupling with 3-Methyl-2-Benzothiazoline Hydrazone. *Anal. Chem.* 41:1750.

Gauntlett, R. B. and R. F. Packham. 1973. The Use of Activated Carbon in Water Treatment. In: Proc. Conference on Activated Carbon in Water Treatment, University of Reading, Water Research Association, Medmenham, England.

Gerber, N. N. 1974. Microbiological Production of Geosmin. EPA-670/2-74-094, U. S. Environmental Protection Agency, Cincinnati, OH.

Gerber, N. N. 1967. Geosmin, an Earthy-Smelling Substance Isolated from Actinomycetes. *Biotech. and Bioeng.* 9:321.

Gerber, N. N. and H. A. Lechevalier. 1965. Geosmin, an Earthy-Smelling Substance Isolated from Actinomycetes. *Appl. Microbiol.* 13:935.

Gjessing, E. T. 1976. Physical and Chemical Characteristics of Aquatic Humus. Ann Arbor Science Publishers, Ann Arbor, MI.

Glaze, W. H. and J. E. Henderson. 1975. Formation of Organochlorine Compounds from the Chlorination of a Municipal Secondary Effluent. *Jour. Water Poll. Control Fed.* 47:2511.

Handbook of Chemistry and Physics. 1967. 48th Ed., Chemical Rubber Co., Cleveland, OH.

Herzing, D. R., V. L. Snoeyink and N. F. Wood. 1977. Activated Carbon Adsorption of the Odorous Compounds 2-Methylisoborneol and Geosmin. *Jour. Amer. Water Works Assoc.* 69:223.

Jain, J. S. and V. L. Snoeyink. 1973. Adsorption from Bisolute Systems on Active Carbon. *Jour. Water Poll. Control Fed.* 45:2463.

Jenkins, D. 1973. Effects of Organic Compounds - Taste, Odor, Color, and Chelation. In: Proc. 15th Water Quality Conference, *Organic Matter in Water Supplies: Occurrence, Significance and Control* (V. L. Snoeyink, ed.), University of Illinois, Urbana, IL. 70:15.

Kaiser, K. L. E. and B. G. Oliver. 1976. Determination of Volatile Halogenated Hydrocarbons in Water by Gas Chromatography. *Anal. Chem.* 48:2207.

Kikuchi, T., T. Mimura, Y. Itoh, Y. Moriwaki, K. Negoro, Y. Masada and T. Inoue. 1973a. Odorous Metabolites of Actinomycetes, Biwake-C and -D Strain Isolated from the Bottom Deposits of Lake Biwa. Identification of Geosmin, 2-Methylisoborneol, and Furfural. *Chem. and Pharm. Bull.* 21:2339.

Kikuchi, T., T. Mimura, K. Haranaya, H. Yano, T. Arinoto, Y. Masada and T. Inoue. 1973b. Odorous Metabolite of Blue-Green Algae: *Schizothrix meulleri* nageli Collected in the Southern Basin of Lake Biwa. Identification of Geosmin. *Chem. and Pharm. Bull.* 21:2342.

Korenman, Y. 1974. Distribution of Chlorophenols between Organic Solvents and Water. *Jour. Appl. Chem.* - USSR. 47:9 (part 2).

Kühn, W. and H. Sontheimer. 1973a. Several Investigations on Activated Charcoal for the Determination of Organic Chloro Compounds. *Vom Wasser.* 41:65.

Kühn, W. and H. Sontheimer. 1973b. Analytic Determination of Chlorinated Organic Compounds with Temperature Programmed Pyrohydrolysis. *Vom Wasser.* 41:1.

Langmuir, I. 1918. The Adsorption of Gases on Plane Surfaces of Glass, Mica and Platinum. *Jour. Amer. Chem. Soc.* 40:1361.

Lee, C. F. 1967. Kinetics of Reactions Between Chlorine and Phenolic Compounds. In: *Principles and Applications of Water Chemistry* (S. Faust and J. Hunter, eds.), Wiley and Sons, Inc., New York.

Leenheer, J. A. and E. D. W. Huffman. 1976. Classification of Organic Solutes in Water Using Macroreticular Resins. Submitted to *Jour. of Research* for publication.

Lenz, V. W. 1911. Zur Prufung des Kampfers. *Archiv. der Pharmazie.* 249:286.

Love, O. T., Jr., G. G. Robeck, J. M. Symons and R. W. Buelow. 1973. Experience with Activated Carbon in the U.S.A. Proc. Conference on Activated Carbon in Water Treatment, University of Reading, Water Research Association, Medmenham, England. p. 279.

Malkonen, P. 1964. *Ann. Acad. Sci. Fennicae Ser. AII.* No. 128.

McCaull, J. and J. Crossland. 1974. *Water Pollution* (B. Commoner, ed.), Harcourt Brace Jovanovich, Inc., New York.

McCreary, J. J. and V. L. Snoeyink. 1977. Granular Activated Carbon in Water Treatment. *Jour. Amer. Water Works Assoc.*, in press.

McGinnes, P. R. and V. L. Snoeyink. 1974. Determination of the Fate of Polynuclear Aromatic Hydrocarbons in Natural Water Systems. Res. Rept. No. 80, Water Resources Center, University of Illinois at Urbana-Champaign, Urbana, IL.

Medsker, L. L., D. Jenkins and J. F. Thomas. 1968. Odorous Compounds in Natural Waters: An Earthy-Smelling Compound Associated with Blue-Green Algae and Actinomycetes. *Environ. Sci. and Technol.* 2:461.

Medsker, L. L., D. Jenkins, J. F. Thomas and C. Koch. 1969. Odorous Compounds in Natural Waters: 2-exo-hydroxy-2-methylbornane, the Major Odorous Compound Produced by Several Actinomycetes. *Environ. Sci. and Technol.* 3:476.

Nakanishi, K. 1962. *Infrared Absorption Spectroscopy*, Holden-Day, Inc., San Francisco, p. 24.

Narkis, N. and M. Rebhun. 1975. The Mechanism of Flocculation Processes in the Presence of Humic Substances. *Jour. Amer. Water Works Assoc.* 67:101.

Pharmacia. 1974. Sephadex: Gel Filtration in Theory and Practice. Upplands Grafiska AB, Sweden.

Piet, G. J., C. J. Zoetman and J. A. Kraayeveld. 1972. Earthy-Smelling Substances in Surface Waters of the Netherlands. *Proc. Soc. Water Treat. and Exam.* 21:281.

Robeck, G. G. 1975. Evaluation of Activated Carbon. Water Supply Research Laboratory, National Environmental Research Center, Cincinnati, OH.

Rook, J. J. 1976. Haloforms in Drinking Water. *Jour. Amer. Water Works Assoc.* 68:168.

Rosen, A. A., C. I. Mashni and R. S. Safferman. 1970. Recent Developments in the Chemistry of Odor in Water: The Cause of Earthy-Musty Odor. *Proc. Water Treat. and Exam.* 10:106.

Safferman, R. S., A. A. Rosen, C. I. Mashni and M. E. Morris. 1967. Earthy-Smelling Substance from a Blue-Green Algae. *Environ. Sci. and Technol.* 1:429.

Schnitzer, M. and S. U. Khan. 1972. *Humic Substances in the Environment,* Marcel Dekker, Inc., New York.

Schweer, K. H., F. Fuchs and H. Sontheimer. 1975. Untersuchungen zur Summarischen Bestimmung von Organisch Gebundenem Schwefel in Wassern und auf Aktivkohlen. *Vom Wasser.* 45:29.

Sigworth, E. A. 1957. Control of Taste and Odor in Water Supplies. *Jour. Amer. Water Works Assoc.* 49:1507.

Silvey, J. K. G., D. E. Henley, R. Hoehn and W. C. Nuney. 1976. Musty-Earthy Odors and Their Biological Control. Proc. Conference on Water Quality, Atlanta, Dec. 1975, AWWA, Denver, CO.

Snoeyink, V. L., W. J. Weber and H. B. Mark. 1969. Sorption of Phenol and Nitrophenol by Active Carbon. *Environ. Sci. and Technol.* 3:918.

Sontheimer, H. 1974. Use of Activated Carbon in Water Treatment Practice and its Regeneration. Special Subject No. 3, Lehrstuhl fur Wasserchemie der Universitat Karlsruhe, Karlsruhe, West Germany.

Sontheimer, H. and D. Maier. 1972. Untersuchungen zur Verbesserung der Trinkwasseraufbereitungstechnologie am Niederrhein (1. Bericht). *Gas und Wasserfach Wasser/Abwasser.* 113:187.

Stahl, E. (ed.). 1969. *Thin-Layer Chromatography.* Springer-Verlag, New York. p. 224.

Standard Methods for the Examination of Water and Wastewater. 1975. 14th Edition, American Public Health Association, Washington, D.C.

Stevens, A. A. and J. M. Symons. 1977. Measurement of Trihalomethane and Precursor Concentration Changes Occurring during Water Treatment and Distribution. Accepted by *Jour. Amer. Water Works Assoc.* for publication, October 1977.

Stevens, A. A., C. J. Slocum, D. R. Seeger and G. G. Robeck. 1976. Chlorination of Organics in Drinking Water. *Jour. Amer. Water Works Assoc.* 68:615.

Stevenson, F. J. 1965. Gross Chemical Fractionation of Organic Matter. In: *Methods of Soil Analysis*, Part 2, Agronomy Monograph #9 (C. A. Black *et al.*, eds.), American Society of Agronomy, Madison, WI, p. 1409

Symons, J. M. 1976. Interim Treatment Guide for the Control of Chloroform and Other Trihalomethanes. Water Supply Research Division, Municipal Environmental Research Laboratory, Environmental Protection Agency, Cincinnati, OH.

Toivonen, H. 1968. Uber Die Reaktionen Des 2-Methylisoborneols und der 2-Methylfenchols in Konzentrierter Salpetersaure. *Tetrahedron Letters.* p. 3041.

U.S. Environmental Protection Agency. 1971. Methods for Organic Pesticides in Water and Wastewater. National Environmental Research Center, Cincinnati, OH.

U.S. Environmental Protection Agency. 1975. Preliminary Assessment of Suspected Carcinogens in Drinking Water - Interior Report to Congress. Office of Toxic Substances, Washington, D.C.

Ward, T. M. and F. W. Getzen. 1969. A Model for the Adsorption of Weak Electrolytes on Solids as a Function of pH--1. *Jour. Colloid and Interface Sci.* 31:441.

Ward, T. M. and F. W. Getzen. 1970. Influence of pH on the Adsorption of Aromatic Acids on Activated Carbon. *Environ. Sci. and Technol.* 4:64.

Weber, W. J., Jr. and J. C. Morris. 1964. Adsorption in Heterogeneous Aqueous Systems. *Jour. Amer. Water Works Assoc.* 56:447.

Zeiss, M. M. and D. A. Pease. 1956. Chromate Esters. II. Reactions of Di-2-Methylfenchyl Chromate. *Jour. Amer. Chem. Soc.* 78:3182.

Zelinsky, N. 1901. Uber eine Synthese der Cyclischentertiaren Alkohole mit Hulfe von Magnesiumhalogenalkylen. *Ber. Dtsch. Chem. Ges.* 34:2877.

Zogorski, J. S. and S. D. Faust. 1974. Removal of Phenols from Polluted Waters. New Jersey Water Resources Research Institute, Rutgers Univ.

Zogorski, J. S. and S. D. Faust. 1976. The Effect of Phosphate Buffer on the Adsorption of 2,4-Dichlorophenol and 2,4-Dinitrophenol. *Jour. Environ. Sci. Health.* A11 (8&9):501.

TECHNICAL REPORT DATA
(Please read Instructions on the reverse before completing)

1. REPORT NO. EPA-600/2-77-223	2.	3. RECIPIENT'S ACCESSION NO.
4. TITLE AND SUBTITLE ACTIVATED CARBON ADSORPTION OF TRACE ORGANIC COMPOUNDS		5. REPORT DATE December 1977 (Issuing Date)
		6. PERFORMING ORGANIZATION CODE
7. AUTHOR(S) Vernon L. Snoeyink, John J. McCreary and Carol J. Murin		8. PERFORMING ORGANIZATION REPORT NO.
9. PERFORMING ORGANIZATION NAME AND ADDRESS Dept. of Civil Engineering University of Illinois Urbana, Illinois 61801		10. PROGRAM ELEMENT NO. 1CC614
		11. CONTRACT/GRANT NO. R-803473
12. SPONSORING AGENCY NAME AND ADDRESS Municipal Environmental Research Laboratory- Cin., OH Office of Research and Development U.S. Environmental Protection Agency Cincinnati, Ohio 45268		13. TYPE OF REPORT AND PERIOD COVERED Final, 1/6/75 to 7/5/77
		14. SPONSORING AGENCY CODE EPA/600/14

15. SUPPLEMENTARY NOTES

Project Officer: Alan A. Stevens, 513/684-7228

16. ABSTRACT

Research was conducted to determine how effectively humic substances and the trace contaminants 2-methylisoborneol (MIB), geosmin, the chlorophenols and polynuclear aromatic hydrocarbons were adsorbed by activated carbon under the competitive adsorption conditions encountered in natural waters. Humic substances compete with MIB and geosmin for adsorption sites on activated carbon and significantly reduce its capacity for these compounds. These naturally occurring odorous compounds were found to be much more strongly adsorbed than the humic substances.

Both the chlorophenols and the polynuclear aromatic hydrocarbons are very strongly adsorbed. Strong competition was observed between anionic and neutral species of 2,4-dichlorophenol and 2,4,6-trichlorophenol. The presence of the various humic substances caused a significant reduction in chlorophenol adsorption capacity. Humic acid did not interfere with the rate of adsorption of a model polynuclear aromatic hydrocarbon, anthracene.

17.	KEY WORDS AND DOCUMENT ANALYSIS	
a. DESCRIPTORS	b. IDENTIFIERS/OPEN ENDED TERMS	c. COSATI Field/Group
Activated Carbon Treatment, Potable Water, Odor Control, Organic Compounds, Actinomyces	Competitive Adsorption, Humic Acids, Chlorophenols, Geosmin, Methylisoborneol, Taste and Odor	13 B
18. DISTRIBUTION STATEMENT Release to Public	19. SECURITY CLASS *(This Report)* Unclassified	21. NO. OF PAGES 126
	20. SECURITY CLASS *(This page)* Unclassified	22. PRICE

Lightning Source UK Ltd.
Milton Keynes UK
UKHW030647240121
377569UK00005B/646